WTF?! NO ONE TOLD ME THIS..

Mental Health for Beginners 101 Guide

NIKKI MAY

Contents

Introduction

So, there I was, in the middle of a chaotic shift, trying to patch up a guy who thought he could take on a lamppost with nothing but a bicycle. Spoiler alert: lampposts always win. I patched him up, cracked a few jokes, and sent him on his merry way. I was the go-to gal for comic relief even in the most serious of situations. Humour was my trusty sidekick, my shield in a world full of chaos. But here's the kicker: beneath all that laughter, I was slowly unravelling.

In those moments, something was whispering at the back of my mind, telling me that not everything was fine. But I ignored it, like when you hear a weird noise in your car and crank up the radio volume to drown it out. Until one day, while juggling life post Ambulance Service and now as a constable in the UK Police, I had to face it. I discovered I had PTSD and depression. It was like finding out your emotional airbags had deployed long ago, and you've been driving with a crumpled front end ever since.

This book is for those of you who are hearing those whispers —or maybe even loud shouts—about your own mental health. Think of it as a beginner's guide, a friendly manual to help you service the complicated vehicle that is your mind. You wouldn't drive your car for years without a check-up, so why do it with your mental health?

Let's face it: life can feel like a constant pressure cooker, and if you're an adult trying to juggle work, family, and maybe the occasional existential crisis, you're not alone. Perhaps you don't fully understand what mental health is, or you're scared to talk about it. Heck, you might not even know where to start. That's where this book comes in.

I've seen firsthand the toll that stress and anxiety can take on a person. My background in emergency services has given me a front-row seat to human crises. And my personal journey has taught me that mental health is just as important as phys- ical health. This book is a product of those experiences, a mix of what I've learned and what I wish someone had told me.

Throughout these pages, we'll explore some key themes together. We'll talk about the importance of checking in with yourself and others. We'll dive into why talking openly about mental health can be a lifesaver. And we'll confront the dangers of untreated depression and the shadow of suicidal thoughts. This isn't just a bunch of fancy words; it's a conver- sation we need to have.

I promise this book isn't just a dry lecture. It's filled with real- life examples and practical strategies that you can apply to your life. Think of it as a tool kit, full of relatable stories and down-to-earth advice. Whether you're dealing with a mental health hiccup or a full-blown meltdown, there's something in here for you.

By the end of this book, you'll have a better understanding of mental health, some practical tools for self-care, and a bit of encouragement to seek professional help if needed. My goal is to help you feel motivated and hopeful about making positive changes. And let's be honest, we could all use a bit more hope in our lives.

So, here's my invitation to you: let's take this journey together. Keep an open mind as we explore the ins and outs of mental health. Take proactive steps toward understanding and improving your well-being. You're not alone in this. We're in it together, and I promise, there's light at the end of the tunnel.

ONE

Starting Your Mental Health Journey

Have you ever tried to assemble flat-pack furniture without instructions? Maybe you ended up with a bookshelf that looked more like modern art. Life without understanding mental health can feel a bit like that—confusing, frustrating, and occasionally resulting in a piece that doesn't quite fit. I remember a time when I thought I had it all together, cracking jokes and handling emergencies like a pro. But inside, I was as lost as a cat in a dog park. It turns out, mental health is a lot like those instruction manuals—essential (oops, there's that word) for getting things right, but often shoved to the back of the drawer until things start wobbling.

Mental Health 101: The Basics You Need to Know

Let's start with the basics. Mental health isn't just about avoiding a meltdown or keeping your cool when someone cuts you off in traffic. It's the whole kit and caboodle, encompassing emotional, psychological, and social well-being. Think of it as the trio of mental gymnasts, each flipping and twisting in perfect harmony when things are going well. But when one of them falters, the whole routine can come crashing down. Your mental health influences how you handle stress, relate to others, and make choices. It's as crucial as keeping your physical health in check—after all, you wouldn't ignore a sprained ankle, so why overlook your mental health?

Now, let's talk about some common misconceptions. Many people think mental health is synonymous with mental illness, but they're as different as a sunroof and a convertible. While mental illness refers to conditions that affect mostly the hardware of your mind, mental health is more about the software and maintaining a balanced, fulfilling life. It's about feeling good, or at least okay, most of the time. It's about bouncing back from setbacks and maintaining relationships without feeling like you're scaling Mount Everest. Mental health isn't just a buzzword; it's a fundamental aspect of overall wellness. By keeping it healthy, you're doing yourself a world of favours.

Awareness is your first line of defence in the mental health arena. It's like checking your car's oil before a long road trip. You don't want to be halfway to nowhere with smoke billowing from the engine. Recognizing early signs of mental health issues can prevent a minor hiccup from turning into a full-blown crisis. Are you feeling unusually tired, irritable, or withdrawn? Those might be your mind's way of saying, "Hey, can we talk?" Being in tune with these signals can make a massive difference in maintaining your well-being. It's not about being hyper-vigilant, but rather being mindful of what's going on inside of you.

Speaking of talking, let's break the ice. Mental health conversations are like the awkward first dance at a wedding—necessary but often avoided. But here's the truth: talking about mental health can be a lifesaver. We need to normalize these conversations, turning them from whispers in the hallway to topics as common as discussing the weather. Stigma has silenced too many people for too long. By opening up, we chip away at the walls of misunderstanding and fear that have kept mental health in the shadows. It's time to bring it into the light, where we can address it openly and honestly.

Reflection Exercise: Start the Conversation

Take a moment to jot down your thoughts on mental health or simply reflect. I hate the workbook-type books, too. What does it mean to you? Have you ever felt hesitant to talk about it? What would make it easier to discuss these topics with friends or family? Consider sharing your reflections with someone you trust.

In this chapter, we've just begun to scratch the surface of mental health. It's a vast and multifaceted topic, but starting with the basics sets the foundation for everything else. Remember, understanding mental health is like having that instruction manual for life's flat-pack challenges. It won't solve every problem, but it certainly helps keep things from toppling over.

Overcoming Information Overload: Where to Begin

Ever felt like you're drowning in a sea of information? It's like standing in the cereal aisle trying to choose between a hundred different boxes when all you really want is a simple bowl of cornflakes. The same thing happens with mental health information. There's an avalanche of data out there, and not all of it is as nutritious as it claims. But here's the trick: it's all about prioritizing. First off, you need to identify credible sources. Think of it like choosing the right ingredients for a dish; you want the freshest, most reliable options. Sources such as reputable mental health organizations, academic journals, and certified professionals are your go-to. Avoid those clickbait articles that promise to cure all your woes with a single magic pill. Differentiate between what's trustworthy and what's just noise. It's like spotting a fake designer bag amidst the real ones—if it looks too good to be true, it probably is.

Now, let's cut through the clutter and create a focused approach. Imagine trying to read every book in the library at once. Overwhelming, right? Instead, set specific mental health goals. Maybe you are keen to learn about managing anxiety or improving your emotional resilience. Whatever it is, focus on that one thing at a time. It's like planting a garden; you can't grow everything all at once, but you can start with a few seeds and nurture them. Schedule regular mental health check-ins, just like you would with a fitness routine. It's your way of keeping track of progress without feeling like you're running a marathon without a map.

Technology can be your best friend or your worst enemy, depending on how you use it. We all know the rabbit hole that is social media, where you go in to check one thing and emerge two hours later, questioning your life choices and then just buying a new sofa. But when used wisely, it's a fantastic tool for mental health learning. Apps like Headspace or Calm can guide you through meditation exercises, while platforms like BetterHelp or Mindvalley offer virtual therapy sessions. These aren't just trendy gadgets but practical tools designed to streamline your mental health journey. And let's not forget online communities that provide support and shared experiences. They're like book clubs but for your mind.

Interactive Element: Curate Your Mental Health Feed

Take a moment to review your digital consumption. What websites, apps, or social media accounts do you follow that positively affect your mental health? Try a cyber clear out of what's worth keeping, and consider unfollowing or unsubscribing from sources that overwhelm you. This small step can create a more focused and supportive digital environment.

But let's be honest; the digital world can be overwhelming. Getting lost scrolling through endless articles, videos, and opinions is easy. So, how do you filter out the noise? Start by setting boundaries. Limit your screen time and choose when and where you consume information. Think of it like setting office hours for your brain. When it's time to switch off, do it without guilt. Curate your mental health content by subscribing to newsletters from trusted experts or joining forums where constructive discussions happen. It's all about creating a space that supports rather than overwhelms.

So there you have it, a way to navigate the vast ocean of mental health information without getting swept away. It's about knowing what to focus on, using technology to your advantage, and filtering out unnecessary noise.

Debunking Myths: Separating Fact from Fiction

Let's face it: myths about mental health are as common as those dodgy ads promising to grow your hair back overnight. They're everywhere, and they can be surprisingly convincing. Take the myth that "mental health issues are rare." It's as if folks believe mental health struggles are the unicorns of health problems, only seen by a select unlucky few. The truth is that mental health issues are as common as Monday mornings. According to the World Health Organization, over 264 million people worldwide suffer from depression alone. Imagine if we all wore a badge—there'd be many of us flashing around the same one. And then there's the whopper that "therapy is only for severe cases." It's like thinking the gym is only for bodybuilders. In reality, therapy is a tool for everyone, offering guidance whether you're dealing with everyday stress or more profound issues. It's not exclusive; it's inclusive and can be a game-changer for anyone willing to try it.

These myths aren't just harmless misunderstandings. They carry weight, casting shadows that make mental health issues seem more taboo than they are. When people buy into these myths, it becomes harder to reach out for help. The stigma surrounding mental health issues builds walls that can feel impossible to scale. Imagine feeling like you need therapy but thinking, "My problems aren't big enough for that," or, "What would people think?" These thoughts create barriers that prevent many from getting the support they need, leading to prolonged suffering. It's like having a leaky roof and convincing yourself it's fine until the whole ceiling caves in. Stigmatization isolates individuals, making them feel like they're fighting a battle no one else understands. Feel it; yeah, I did too.

But here's where we must step up and arm ourselves with facts. Evidence-based information is the light that dispels these shadows. Studies indicate that mental health issues cut across all walks of life. They're not picky about who they affect, and they don't care about your background, intelligence, or social status. Early intervention through therapy can be as effective for mental health as regular exercise is for physical health. It's about maintaining well-being, not just addressing problems when they become unmanageable. By understanding this, we open doors to treatment and recovery that were previously locked by ignorance.

To combat these myths, we need to sharpen our critical thinking skills. It's like equipping ourselves with a mental toolkit to dismantle misinformation. Start by asking questions when you come across mental health claims. Who is saying this? What's their agenda? Where's the evidence? Are there multiple sources that confirm the same thing? This isn't just about being sceptical; it's about being informed. Relying on a single source is like balancing on a one-legged stool—wobbly at best. Multiple perspectives give you a broader, more balanced view, allowing you to confidently separate fact from fiction.

In a world where myths can spread faster than viral memes, it's crucial to be vigilant about what we accept as truth. By challenging these myths, we do more than just correct misconceptions; we pave the way for open conversations and a more supportive environment for those facing mental health challenges. It's about building a foundation of under-standing that supports everyone, whether they're scaling mountains or just trying to get through the day.

Building Your Mental Health Toolkit

Imagine trying to fix a leaky faucet with nothing but a tooth-pick and some duct tape. Jason Bourne or the A-Team would probably be the only ones capable. Pretty frustrating, right? That's what tackling mental health without the right tools can feel like. But don't worry, I've got you covered. Let's start with journaling. Think of it as a way to chat with yourself on paper, where you can spill your thoughts without judgment. It's not just for angsty teens; it's a powerful tool for emotional processing. Whether you're jotting down how you felt during the day or scribbling random thoughts, it helps make sense of the chaos swirling in your mind. Plus, it's cheaper than ther-apy, and you don't have to leave your couch.

Next up, mindfulness and meditation. Now, before you roll your eyes, hear me out. This isn't about sitting cross-legged chanting "om" for hours. It's about taking a moment to breathe, to be present, and to let the world slow down a bit. Even a few minutes of focusing on your breath can do wonders for calming a racing mind. Think of it as a mental reset button. And if you're sceptical, there are apps out there to guide you. Headspace and Calm are popular picks for beginners, offering bite-sized sessions that fit into any schedule. It's like having a pocket-sized guru, minus the incense.

We can't discuss mental health tools without mentioning cognitive-behavioral techniques. This might sound a bit clinical, but bear with me. CBT is about changing the way you think to change how you feel. It's like upgrading your mental software. If you catch yourself spiralling into negative thoughts, CBT helps you reframe those thoughts into something more balanced. It's the mental equivalent of turning lemons into lemonade. And the best part? You can learn some CBT techniques yourself through workbooks or online resources, giving you the power to shift your mindset without needing a PhD.

Now, let's add some practical exercises to your toolkit. Ever tried a daily gratitude practice? It's as simple as jotting down three things you're grateful for each day or just saying them in your mind as soon as you wake up or when you're brushing your teeth. It sounds cheesy, but it's like training your brain to spot the silver linings. Over time, it can shift your focus from what's wrong to what's right. And when stress creeps in, there's nothing like a good breathing exercise. Deep, slow breaths can signal your brain to chill out, lowering stress in a flash. It's like telling your mind, "Hey, we've got this."

But even with all these tools, none of it means much without a solid support system. Think of your friends and family as the scaffolding that holds you up when things get wobbly. Building a network of supportive folks isn't just nice; it's crucial. Studies show that having people you can lean on boosts resilience and mental health. So, don't hesitate to reach out to those who lift you. And remember, support doesn't just come from loved ones. Community resources, support groups, and even AI on your computer or phone can be a resource to reach out to, or online forums can connect you with others who understand what you're going through.

Your toolkit is a personal thing, kind of like a music playlist tailored just for you. Feel free to customize it. Not a fan of journaling? Try voice memos or drawing. Meditation, not your jam? Take a mindful walk instead. The key is to adapt these tools to fit your needs and lifestyle. Track what works and what doesn't, and don't be afraid to make adjustments along the way or mix and match. Meditation whilst walking, repeating your grateful statements for the day, or mindfulness whilst having a coffee at work. CBT eating breakfast or whilst using the toilet. Whatever works for you is the point; after all, this is your mental health we're talking about, and you deserve a toolkit that fits like a glove.

Understanding Your Mental Health Baseline

Let's talk baselines. Not the kind you find in a song or a sports field, but the mental health variety. Think of it as your mind's personal status report. It's the point of reference that helps you understand what's normal for you on any given day. By knowing your mental health baseline, you can spot when things start to veer off course, just like noticing your car's gas gauge dipping toward empty. Your baseline includes indicators like your usual energy levels, mood stability, and how you handle stress. It's your mental health's homeostasis, the sweet spot where things feel balanced. Understanding this helps you gauge when you're running low on emotional fuel, so to speak.

Assessing your current mental health state doesn't require a degree in psychology or a fancy diagnostic tool. It's more about tuning in to your internal radio station. One way to do this is through mood tracking. This isn't just jotting down "happy" or "sad" each day. It's about noticing patterns and fluctuations over time. Apps like Daylio or Moodfit can help you track your mood, offering insights into how different factors—like sleep, diet, and social interactions—affect your mental state. Another method is self-reflection, where you take a few moments each day to ponder how you're feeling and why. Self-reflection prompts can guide you through this process, asking questions like, "What's one thing that went well today?" or "What felt challenging?" Some smartphones have this sort of app available for health tracking straight out of the box.

Monitoring changes over time is crucial because mental health is fluid; it ebbs and flows like the tide. Keeping a mental health diary can be a game-changer here. It's like having your own personal archive of thoughts, feelings, and experiences. By jotting down regular entries, you create a narrative that highlights trends and triggers. Maybe you'll notice that certain situations consistently elevate your stress levels or that your mood dips every time you skip breakfast. Recognizing these patterns enables you to take proactive steps to manage your mental health more effectively. It's like having a roadmap that helps you navigate the ups and downs.

Establishing healthy benchmarks is the next step. It's about setting realistic mental health goals based on your baseline and the patterns you've observed. Think of these benchmarks as the mental equivalent of fitness goals. Maybe your first goal is to maintain a steady mood throughout the workweek, or to reduce the frequency of anxious thoughts. Whatever they are, ensure they're achievable and tailored to your needs. And when you reach these goals, celebrate them. Small victories in mental health are akin to levelling up in a game. Each achievement, no matter how minor it seems, is a testament to your progress and resilience.

Understanding your mental health baseline is like having a compass in an unpredictable world. It guides you toward a better understanding of yourself and helps you maintain balance. By assessing your current state, monitoring changes, and setting achievable goals, you create a personalized framework for mental well-being. This isn't just a one-time exercise but an ongoing practice that evolves with you. As you grow and change, so will your baseline, reflecting the dynamic nature of mental health. Through this awareness and adaptability, you equip yourself to face whatever life throws your way with confidence and clarity.

How to Navigate the Sea of Mental Health Resources

Picture this: you're standing in the middle of a gigantic library, surrounded by towering shelves filled with books, videos, and podcasts, each promising the golden key to mental health. Overwhelming, right? But navigating these resources doesn't have to feel like finding a needle in a haystack or, worse, a needle in a pile of other needles. It's more like being a savvy shopper in a bustling market—knowing what to pick and what to pass by. In the realm of books, start with authors who have credentials or a track record that speaks volumes. Maybe they're therapists, psychologists, or have lived experiences that lend them credibility. Online articles are trickier; always check for the source's reputation and whether they cite reliable studies. Podcasts and videos? They're the snackable content of the mental health world, perfect for when you're on the move. Look for those hosted by experts or featuring guest appearances from people who know their stuff.

Evaluating the quality of these resources is like being a detective—minus the trench coat and magnifying glass. Start with a quick background check on the author. Google is your friend here. What's their professional background? Have they published other works that have been well-received? Next, dive into the reviews. Reader feedback can offer you insights that a book cover won't. You're likely on the right track if a resource is consistently praised for its depth and clarity. On the flip side, if you see a pattern of negative reviews pointing out inaccuracies or lack of depth, it's probably best to steer clear. Remember, the aim is to find resources that are not just informative but are also grounded in reality.

Matching resources to your needs is a bit like tailoring a suit. You want something that fits you just right. If you're grappling with anxiety, seek out resources specifically designed for anxiety management. If you're curious about mindfulness, there's a wealth of content dedicated to that, too. The key is to define your personal mental health goals and align your reading or listening materials with them. For instance, if your goal is to improve sleep, you might look into Calm's sleep stories or a book about sleep hygiene. Tailor your resource intake to address your unique mental health conditions or goals, ensuring the support you receive is directly relevant to your needs.

Continued learning in mental health isn't just a one-time event; it's a lifelong process. Think of it like keeping your wardrobe updated with the latest trends. The field of mental health is constantly evolving, with new research and developments emerging regularly. Staying informed can empower you to make better decisions about your mental health. Engage with new material, attend workshops, or join forums where the latest discussions take place. This ongoing education helps you adapt to changes and challenges, equipping you with the knowledge to navigate life's ups and downs more effectively.

The beauty of mental health resources is that they're varied and abundant, offering a tapestry of knowledge waiting to be explored. Whether it's through the wisdom of a well-written book, the insights of a compelling podcast, or the guidance of an informative video, there's something out there for every-one. With the right approach, these resources can illuminate your path, offering clarity and understanding in a world that often feels confusing and overwhelming. So, keep your curiosity alive, and continue seeking out the information that resonates with you. Together, these resources form a founda-tion of support that can help you build a healthier, happier life.

TWO

Developing Practical Self-Care Strategies

I magine you're a smartphone. No, really, go with me on this. You buzz along, multitasking, keeping all the apps running smoothly, until suddenly, you're down to 1% battery, desperately searching for a charger. That's us, my friend, when we neglect self-care. Self-care is the charging cable we often forget we need, but it's crucial for keeping our mental health battery full. It's not just spa days and bubble baths, though those are delightful. It's about maintaining our mental health, like regularly fueling our bodies and minds with what they need to function well. Self-care is vital (and I mean vital) for reducing stress and improving overall well-being, as it's linked to better self-esteem and optimism, according to Psychology Today (source 1).

Now, I know what you're thinking: "Who has time for self-care between work, family, and Netflix binges?" Let's break it down into bite-sized chunks that fit into even the busiest of schedules. Start with a five-minute breathing exercise.

Yes, just five minutes. Sit comfortably, close your eyes, and inhale deeply through your nose. Hold it for a few seconds, then exhale slowly. Repeat this a few times, and voilà, you've just given your brain a mini-vacation. It's like hitting the reset button, allowing stress to melt away, if only for a moment.

Another quick win? Gratitude journaling before bed. Keep a notebook on your bedside table and jot down three things you're thankful for each day. It doesn't have to be monu-mental—"I didn't spill coffee on my shirt today" works just fine. This simple practice shifts your focus from what's wrong to what's right, setting a positive tone for your dreams. It's like planting seeds of optimism that bloom into resilience over time. You might be surprised how such a small habit can reshape your outlook.

Life loves to throw curveballs, so let's talk about flexibility in self-care. Imagine trying to do yoga in a straightjacket—not ideal, right? That's what rigid self-care routines can feel like. Instead, adapt your practices to suit your circumstances. If a work deadline looms, maybe your yoga class turns into a few quick stretches at your desk. The key is to weave self-care into your existing activities rather than adding it to your to-do list. It's like sneaking veggies into a kid's meal.

Explore these resources to boost your self-care game:

- **Headspace**: An app for guided meditation and relaxation, perfect for those five-minute breaks.
- **Calm**: Offers sleep stories and mindfulness exercises to help you unwind.

- **Self-Care Check-In**: An online community where
  you can swap self-care tips and support.

Now that we've got a few self-care practices under our belt, let's talk about resources. You don't need to climb a mountain to find them. They're as accessible as your smartphone. Apps like Headspace and Calm are excellent for guided meditation and relaxation, offering sessions tailored to whatever time you have. And if you're more of a community person, online forums and social media groups are buzzing with self-care tips and support. They're like virtual coffee shops where you can exchange ideas with like-minded folks.

Remember, self-care isn't a one-size-fits-all deal. It's about finding what recharges your mental health battery and incorporating it into your life seamlessly. It's about giving yourself permission to pause and prioritize your well-being, even amidst the chaos. So, grab that metaphorical charging cable and let's get to it.

Creating a Personalized Self-Care Routine

Crafting a self-care routine is like curating your own personal playlist. It should resonate with your unique rhythm, evolving with your needs and preferences. First, identify your personal stressors and figure out what truly helps you decompress. Maybe it's the relentless ping of email notifications or the constant buzz of city life. Recognizing these stressors is the first step to addressing them. Now, think about what genuinely brings you relief. Is it the quiet solitude with a book, or perhaps a brisk walk in the park? Balancing these self-care activities throughout your week isn't just about scheduling; it's about creating moments that allow you to breathe, to pause, and to recharge.

Self-assessment tools can be incredibly helpful in finding what works best for you. Start with some self-reflection exercises. Ask yourself questions like, "What do I need right now?" or "What would make me feel at peace?" This can help you determine your priorities. Sometimes, we don't need another yoga class; we might just need to sit quietly with our thoughts. Journaling is another effective tool. It's not just about writing down what you did, but how each activity made you feel. A simple prompt like, "What self-care activity felt most nourishing today?" can provide insight into what genuinely benefits your mental health. Over time, patterns will emerge, highlighting practices that deserve a permanent spot in your routine.

Consistency is key to making any self-care routine effective. Think of it like brushing your teeth—skipping a day here and there won't ruin everything, but regular practice keeps everything in check. Set realistic self-care goals that fit into your lifestyle. Maybe it's five minutes of meditation each morning or a weekly art class to unleash your creativity. Whatever it is, make sure it's achievable. Creating a weekly self-care schedule can help. Plotting out time slots for different activities ensures you're not just squeezing self-care into the cracks but giving it the priority it deserves. Remember, the goal is not to add stress by over-scheduling, but to create a rhythm that feels natural.

Regularly reviewing and adjusting your routine is just as important as establishing it. Life changes, and so should your self-care practices. Check-in with your progress monthly. Ask yourself, "Is this still working for me?" or "What do I need to tweak?" Being open to trying new practices keeps self-care fresh and responsive to your needs. Maybe you've always done morning jogs, but now evenings feel more relaxing. Or perhaps that pottery class isn't as fulfilling as it used to be. Flexibility is your friend. Adjusting your routine doesn't mean starting from scratch; it's about fine-tuning what's already there to better suit your current situation.

Mindfulness Made Easy: Techniques for Every Day

Mindfulness. You've probably heard it tossed around like a trendy buzzword, but beneath its zen exterior lies a power-house for mental clarity. At its core, mindfulness is about being present in the moment, fully experiencing life without getting tangled in the web of past regrets or future anxieties. Imagine being able to focus on a single task without your mind wandering off like a distracted puppy. That's the magic of mindfulness—it enhances focus and concentration, making even mundane tasks feel more manageable. But it doesn't stop there. Mindfulness can also significantly reduce anxiety and stress, acting like a mental broom, sweeping away the clutter and chaos that often cloud our days.

Let's get practical with some easy mindfulness exercises you can slip into your daily routine. First up, mindful breathing techniques. Find a comfortable spot, close your eyes, and focus on your breath. Feel the air as it enters through your nose, fills your lungs, and exits through your mouth. As you breathe, let go of any tension you're holding in your shoulders, jaw, or wherever stress likes to camp out. It's like each breath is a gentle wave, washing over you and carrying away any worry. Another technique is body scan meditation. Lie down in a quiet space, so maybe not on the bus on the way home from work, and slowly bring your attention to each part of your body, from your toes to the top of your head. Notice any sensations, tension, or discomfort and simply acknowledge them without judgment. It's like giving your body a mental massage, releasing knots you didn't even know you had.

Mindfulness isn't just something you do in a quiet room with candles and soft music. It can be woven into everyday activities, transforming mundane moments into opportunities for peace and clarity. Take eating, for example. Instead of wolfing down your lunch while scrolling through your phone, try practicing mindfulness while eating. Savor each bite, notice the flavors and textures, and appreciate the nourishment it provides. It's like giving your meal the attention it deserves, turning eating into a sensory experience rather than a speed race. And how about mindful walking in nature? Next time you're out for a stroll, leave your phone behind and focus on the sensation of your feet on the ground, the rustle of leaves in the wind, and the rhythm of your breath. It's a simple act, yet it connects you to the world in a way that's both grounding and uplifting; trust me, it really does.

Making mindfulness a habit is where the real challenge lies. It's all too easy to get caught up in the whirlwind of daily life and forget to pause. But like any worthwhile practice, mindfulness flourishes with regular attention. Consider setting reminders for mindfulness breaks throughout your day. Perhaps a gentle chime on your phone or a sticky note on your fridge to nudge you into taking a few mindful moments. Think of it as mental stretching, a way to keep your mind limber and refreshed. Joining mindfulness groups can also provide support and accountability. Whether it's a local meditation circle or an online community, having a group to share experiences and insights can deepen your practice and keep you motivated.

Mindfulness isn't about achieving a state of constant bliss or shutting out the world. It's about opening up to each moment with curiosity and compassion, allowing yourself to fully engage in life as it unfolds. It's a practice that invites you to slow down, breathe, and reconnect with yourself amidst the busyness of everyday life.

Stress Less: Practical Tips for Stress Management

Stress. It's that unwelcome guest who overstays their welcome, turning your life into a whirlwind of anxiety and sleepless nights. Identifying what's causing it is the first step to kicking it to the curb. For many of us, workplace pressures sit at the top of the list. Imagine juggling tasks like a circus performer with a dozen flaming torches—emails, meetings, deadlines, all demanding your attention. It can feel like you're constantly on the edge of dropping it all. Then there's the realm of relationships, where the stakes are high, and the emotions run deep. Whether it's a friend who's become distant or a partner who seems to speak a different language, these challenges can leave you feeling isolated or over-whelmed. Recognizing these stressors is crucial because only then can we begin to tackle them head-on.

Once you know what you're up against, it's time to arm yourself with effective stress management techniques. Let's talk progressive muscle relaxation. This isn't just a fancy term therapists throw around; it's a method that works. Find a quiet spot, take a deep breath, and start by focusing on your toes. Tense them for a few seconds, then slowly release. Move up through your legs, abdomen, arms, and neck, letting each area relax in turn. It's like giving your entire body a spa day, helping release tension you didn't even know you were carrying. Visualization exercises are another powerful tool. Picture yourself on a serene beach, the sun warming your skin, the waves lapping gently at the shore. Visualization allows your mind to escape the chaos, offering a sanctuary where stress can't follow.

Healthy coping mechanisms are your allies in this battle. Physical activity is a well-known stress reliever, not just because it releases endorphins, but because it gives your mind a break from what's troubling you. Whether it's running, yoga, or a brisk walk, moving your body can help reset your brain. And don't underestimate the power of creative outlets like art or music. They're not just hobbies; they're lifelines. When you paint, write, or play an instrument, you express emotions that words can't capture, channeling stress into something beautiful and cathartic.

Regular stress check-ins are like taking your emotional temperature. Keep a stress journal where you jot down your stressors, your reactions, and the strategies you used. This isn't just a record; it's a tool for understanding patterns and triggers. Over time, you'll see what sets you off and helps you calm down. Stress assessment scales can also be helpful, providing a more structured way to evaluate your stress levels. Using these scales, you can track changes over time, identifying when stress might reach unhealthy levels and when it's time to seek extra support. By regularly assessing your stress, you gain control over it rather than letting it control you.

Digital Detox: Reclaiming Your Peace in a Tech-Savvy World

Imagine waking up one morning without immediately reaching for your phone. No notifications, no buzzing, just the soft, unhurried start to a day. In our tech-saturated world, this sounds almost idyllic, doesn't it? But here's the catch: the constant ping of technology, while convenient, can wreak havoc on our mental health. Extensive screen time, especially before bed, has been shown to disrupt sleep, leaving us tossing and turning in the glow of our devices. And let's not forget the sneaky anxiety and comparison game that social media loves to play. You're scrolling through pictures of someone's dream vacation while stuck on your couch with a bowl of cereal. It's enough to make anyone feel like they're missing out on life.

Before you consider tossing your devices out the window, let's talk about a more practical approach: digital detox. This isn't about giving up technology altogether (we're not moving to a cabin in the woods) but regaining control. Start by setting boundaries for screen time. Maybe it's no phones at the dinner table or limiting your evening social media scrolling to 30 minutes. Designate tech-free zones in your home, like the bedroom or dining area, where devices are off-limits. These small changes can create a sanctuary from digital noise, giving you space to breathe and think.

Mindful technology use is another game-changer. It's about being selective and intentional with your screen time. Curate your social media feeds to include content that uplifts and inspires you rather than stuff that makes you feel like you're on the outside looking in. Follow accounts that bring joy, education, or motivation into your life. When it comes to digital interactions, schedule specific times for them. Perhaps you check emails only during work hours or set aside a particular time to catch up with friends online. This approach prevents the constant drip of digital distractions from hijacking your day.

The benefits of reducing screen time are profound. With less digital clutter, you might find your focus sharpening, productivity rising, and even your mood lifting. It's like clearing out a cluttered room—you finally have space to move and breathe. Relationships can also improve when we're not glued to our screens. Conversations become more meaningful when we're fully present, not distracted by the latest meme or notification. Disconnecting from technology, even temporarily, can enhance the quality of life, allowing you to reconnect with the tangible world around you.

Imagine spending a weekend afternoon hiking in the fresh air, your phone tucked away in your pocket, or enjoying a meal with loved ones without the constant interruptions of digital dings. These moments of peace and connection remind us of the beauty and richness of life beyond our screens. Technology has its place but doesn't have to dominate every waking moment. Reclaiming your time and setting boundaries can create a balance that nourishes your mental health and enriches your life.

Sleep Matters: Improving Your Rest for Better Mental Health

We all know that feeling of running on empty when sleep has been more elusive than a unicorn in a forest. Believe it or not, sleep is the unsung hero of mental health. It's the silent partner working behind the scenes to keep your mood and cognition in top shape. When you're sleep-deprived, it's like trying to drive a car with a flat tyre. Everything feels harder and more frustrating than it should be. Your mood can take a nosedive, making you irritable or downright grumpy, and your cognitive abilities, those brainy skills like problem-solving and memory, become sluggish. It's like wading through mental molasses. Sleep helps regulate our emotions, making us better equipped to handle whatever life throws our way. Without it, even the smallest hiccups can feel like insurmountable mountains.

But let's talk about how to get that sweet, restorative sleep. Establishing a consistent bedtime routine is your first step. It's like training a puppy—you need to set a pattern. Try to go to bed and wake up at the same time every day (not so easy for shift workers, I know, but use the sleep routine, even if you can use the time as one), even on weekends. Your body thrives on routine, and a regular sleep schedule can help regulate your internal clock. Creating a sleep-conducive environment is also key. Think of your bedroom as a sanctuary. Keep it cool, dark, and quiet. Block out noise with a white noise machine or earplugs if needed. Ditch the electronics an hour before bed; the blue light from screens can confuse your brain into thinking it's still daytime. Instead, opt for a good book or some calming music to ease you into sleep mode.

Common sleep issues, like insomnia, can feel like battling an invisible enemy. You lie there, staring at the ceiling, willing sleep to come. If this sounds familiar, consider some techniques to help you fall asleep faster. Deep breathing exercises can calm your racing mind. Try the 4-7-8 method: inhale through your nose for a count of four, hold for seven, then exhale through your mouth for eight. It's like a lullaby for your nervous system. For those restless nights, visualization can be your ally. Picture a peaceful, relaxing scene in detail—the sound of waves on a beach, the rustle of leaves in a forest. Let your mind wander there, away from the worries that keep you awake.

Quality sleep doesn't just keep the grumpies at bay; it transforms your day-to-day experience. A good night's rest enhances your mood and energy levels, making you feel like you can take on the world—or at least get through that morning meeting without needing a vat of coffee. Your cognitive functions get a boost, too. Memory becomes sharper, focus more laser-like, and problem-solving skills get a little turbocharge. It's like waking up with a brain that's been to a spa overnight. Good sleep is the foundation upon which all other self-care practices build. Without it, everything else can feel like an uphill struggle.

As we wrap up this chapter on self-care, remember that each of these practices is a piece of the larger puzzle of mental well-being. Sleep, self-care routines, mindfulness—all are interconnected and support the broader goal of maintaining mental health. Next, we'll explore how to build mental resilience and toughness, equipping you with the skills to face life's challenges head-on.

THREE

Building Mental Toughness and Resilience

Picture this: You're standing in the middle of a wild storm, feeling the wind whip around you like a WWE wrestler on a mission. Most of us would rush for cover, but not everyone. Some folks stand tall, their feet planted firmly on the ground, bending like a willow but never breaking. This is resilience in action. Resilience and its trusty sidekick, mental grit, are more than just buzzwords—they're the secret sauce to weathering life's storms without getting washed away. Resilience is about bouncing back from adversity, like a rubber band snapping back into shape after being stretched. And grit? It's the perseverance and passion that keeps you trekking toward your goals, even when the going gets tough. These traits are the silent architects of mental health, helping us maintain balance and sanity when everything around us seems to be spiralling into chaos.

So, what makes someone mentally gritty? Picture a marathon runner, one of those folks who keep pounding the pavement, mile after mile, even when their legs scream to stop (my wife is one of these folks; I'm more of an "I'll run if the house is on fire type). Mentally gritty individuals have a few key traits up their sleeves. They possess emotional control, the ability to keep their cool even when life slings lemons at them like a hyperactive fruit ninja. They're persistent, sticking to their goals with the tenacity of a dog with a bone, refusing to let setbacks derail them. And they're adaptable, shifting their sails to catch the wind when circumstances change. These characteristics form the backbone of resilience, allowing individuals to face adversity head-on without crumbling like a cookie in hot tea.

But how do you build resilience if you're feeling more like a soggy sponge than a sturdy rubber band? Fear not, my friend. The building blocks of resilience are within your reach. Emotional control and regulation are at the foundation, helping you manage emotions like a seasoned air traffic controller guiding planes through turbulent skies. Next, we have persistence and perseverance. Like a climber ascending a steep mountain, every step takes you closer to the peak, even if the path is rocky. And then there's adaptability, the art of bending without breaking, adjusting to life's curveballs with the grace of a ballerina on a bumpy stage.

Now, let's map out a resilience roadmap that'll guide you on this journey. Start by setting realistic and achievable goals. Think of them as stepping stones across a river, each one leading you closer to the other side. These goals should stretch you a bit, but not so much that you feel like you're trying to leap across the Grand Canyon. Develop a positive outlook and attitude, seeing challenges as opportunities for growth rather than insurmountable obstacles. It's like turning a mountain into a molehill, shifting your perspective to ease the climb.

Interactive Element: Journaling Prompt

Grab a journal (it doesn't have to be a journal, a voice note, or a text message to yourself; whatever you need and works for you) and jot down a few realistic goals you'd like to achieve in the next month. Reflect on how these goals align with your values and what steps you can take to reach them. Consider what obstacles might arise and how you can adapt to overcome them.

The beauty of resilience is that it's not a destination but an ongoing personal development process. Journaling your progress can be a powerful tool, capturing your growth like snapshots in an album. Regular self-reflection allows you to adapt and adjust, like a sail of a boat, ensuring that your resilience toolkit evolves as you do. Each entry is a testament to your journey, highlighting the lessons learned and the strengths gained. Remember, resilience isn't about never falling—it's about rising again, stronger and wiser than before.

Bouncing Back: How to Recover from Setbacks

Let's talk about setbacks. They're as inevitable as finding that one sock missing after doing laundry. Those moments are when life throws a wrench in your plans, and you're left standing there, wondering how everything went sideways. It's not a matter of if they'll happen, but when. And when they do, they have a way of shaking your mental health like a snow globe. Emotions can run rampant—frustration, disappointment, and sometimes a hefty dose of self-doubt. It's easy to feel like you're stuck in a loop of failure, but here's the thing: setbacks are temporary. They're like a passing thunderstorm, intense but fleeting, leaving behind clearer skies if you're willing to wait it out.

When setbacks strike, it's crucial to have a game plan for bouncing back. First, develop a support network. Think of it as your personal pit crew, ready to help you get back on track. Surround yourself with people who lift you up, whether it's friends, family, or a mentor who's been through the trenches. They'll offer guidance and perspective, reminding you that you're not alone in this. Practicing self-compassion and forgiveness is another key strategy. It's all too easy to beat yourself up over mistakes, but remember, you're human, not a robot. Give yourself the grace you'd offer a friend. And once you've dusted yourself off, set new, achievable goals. These should be bite-sized and realistic, serving as stepping stones to rebuild your momentum.

Viewing setbacks as learning opportunities might sound like a cliché, but there's wisdom in that dusty old saying. Each setback holds a lesson, like a hidden nugget of wisdom waiting to be uncovered. Reflect on what went wrong and why. Was it a lack of preparation, a miscalculation, or just plain bad luck? Identifying these lessons is like adding tools to your mental toolbox, equipping you for future challenges. Once you've gleaned the insights, apply them moving forward. It's like upgrading your software and refining your approach with each iteration so you're better prepared the next time you face a similar obstacle.

Let's not just talk theory; let's bring in some real-world examples. Take Nick Vujicic, for instance. Born without limbs, Nick faced bullying and discrimination, yet he transformed his setbacks into a powerful message of hope and resilience. Today, he's a motivational speaker, inspiring millions around the world. His story is a testament to the human spirit's capacity to rise above adversity. Or consider Bethany Hamilton, a professional surfer who lost her arm to a shark attack. Instead of giving up, she got back on her board and continued her career, becoming an advocate for shark conservation. Like many everyday heroes in our communities, these individuals show us that setbacks don't define us. It's how we respond that shapes us and the world around us.

In every neighbourhood, there's someone quietly battling their own setbacks, perhaps not making headlines but embodying resilience all the same. It could be the single parent juggling two jobs or the student overcoming learning challenges. Their stories remind us that resilience isn't reserved for the famous. It's a quality found in the fabric of everyday life. These real-world examples prove that bouncing back isn't just possible; it's achievable for anyone willing to look beyond the immediate setback and toward the horizon of possibility. Resilience is a skill, honed through experience, one that grows stronger each time you choose to rise.

Real-Life Resilience: Lessons from Everyday Heroes

Everyday Heroes walk among us, often unnoticed, yet their stories of resilience shine bright in the face of adversity. Take, for instance, the community leader who tirelessly works to bring people together after a devastating natural disaster. They rally volunteers, organize resources, and provide a sense of stability when everything else seems to be falling apart. Their unwavering commitment to rebuilding not only structures but also the spirit of their community exemplifies resilience in action. Or consider the single parent who juggles multiple jobs to keep food on the table and a roof over their children's heads. Despite the challenges, they maintain a positive outlook, teaching their kids the importance of perseverance and love. These are not tales of extraordinary feats but of ordinary people doing extraordinary things, showing us that resilience is not reserved for the few but accessible to us all.

The heart of these stories lies in the lessons they teach us about resilience. First and foremost is the power of hope and optimism. It's the power of belief that better days are ahead, even when the present feels bleak. Hope is the fuel that keeps us going when the road is long and the nights are dark. It's about seeing the possibility of light at the end of the tunnel and moving toward it; it is darkest just before dawn, one step at a time. Community support and collaboration also play pivotal roles. No one faces adversity alone, and these heroes remind us of the strength found in unity. Whether leaning on friends and family or reaching out to neighbours, the collective power of community can lift us from the depths of despair. It's about recognizing that we are stronger and more resilient than we could ever be on our own.

Through these stories, we're encouraged to foster empathy and connection. When we open our hearts to the experiences of others, we find inspiration in their journeys. It reminds us that we are not alone in our struggles and that others have walked similar paths and emerged stronger. This shared human experience builds a bridge of understanding and compassion, allowing us to support one another in meaningful ways. Empathy is the glue that holds us together, helping to cultivate relationships that nurture resilience. By listening to and learning from the stories of others, we gain valuable insights that enrich our lives and encourage us to keep going, even when the going gets tough.

So, how can we apply these lessons in our own lives? One way is by volunteering to support others in need. Whether it's lending a hand at a local shelter or organizing a community event, acts of service not only help those around us but also reinforce our sense of purpose and connection. Practising gratitude for personal strengths is another key takeaway. By acknowledging and appreciating our resilience, we build confidence and fortitude. It's about recognizing the small victories and using them as stepping stones toward greater achievements. Gratitude shifts our focus from what's lacking to what's abundant, fostering a mindset that welcomes challenges as opportunities for growth.

These everyday heroes remind us that resilience is not about never facing challenges, but about rising to meet them with courage and determination. Their stories serve as a beacon, guiding us toward a place where hope and community light the way. They teach us that while life's hurdles may be daunting, they are not insurmountable. With the right mindset and support, we, too, can become heroes in our own right, in our own lives, crafting stories of resilience that inspire and uplift those around us. As we forge ahead, let us carry these lessons with us, embracing the power of resilience to transform our lives and the world around us.

The Power of Perspective: Mindset Shifts for Growth

Imagine waking up and instead of seeing the mountain of tasks ahead as insurmountable, you see them as opportunities to flex your mental muscles. This is the magic of changing your perspective. Our mindset acts like glasses, colouring how we view the world and approach challenges. Shifting from a fixed mindset, where abilities are seen as static, to a growth mindset opens the door to endless possibilities. In a growth or millionaires mindset, failure isn't a dead-end; it's a detour sign pointing the way to new strategies and learning. This shift can transform how you cope with setbacks, turning obstacles into stepping stones toward resilience and personal growth. The relationship between perspective and mental health is profound. A positive perspective can lighten the mental load, making life's hurdles feel like manageable hills rather than towering mountains.

So, how do you change the lens through which you view the world? Start by reframing negative thoughts and beliefs. When you think, "I can't do this," challenge that thought. Ask yourself, "What if I could?" or "What would it take for this to be possible?" This simple shift can turn a brick wall into a temporary roadblock. Practicing gratitude is another powerful technique. By focusing on what you have rather than what you lack, you change your mental focus from scarcity to abundance. Keep a gratitude journal. Write down three things you're grateful for each day. It could be as simple as a sunny morning or a good cup of coffee. This practice rewires your brain to notice the positives, fostering a resilient mindset ready to tackle challenges.

The stories of individuals who have embraced these mindset shifts offer powerful lessons. Consider Carol Dweck's concept of a growth mindset, which emphasizes the idea that abilities can grow with effort and learning from failures. One individual shared how adopting a growth mindset helped them overcome a fear of public speaking. By viewing each speaking opportunity as a chance to improve rather than a test of their worth, they gradually found confidence and even enjoyment in what once terrified them. Another common story involves job loss, where some individuals saw it as a chance to explore new careers, ultimately finding paths more aligned with their passions, and that pretty much explains why I'm here tapping at a keyboard. These transformations highlight how powerful a mindset shift can be, turning what seems like a setback into a springboard for growth and development.

Creating a culture that embraces a growth mindset can amplify these personal transformations. At work, this means encouraging innovation and viewing mistakes as part of the learning process. When teams are open to experimenting and learning from failures, they foster an environment where creativity and resilience thrive. In family settings, promoting open-mindedness helps family members support each other's growth. Encourage discussions about what everyone is learning or struggling with, fostering an atmosphere where growth is celebrated over being "right" or "perfect." By nurturing a growth mindset culture, you create spaces where people feel safe to stretch their limits, try new things, and learn from their experiences without fear of judgment.

Perspective is a powerful tool, and by shifting how we view challenges, we can transform struggles into opportunities for growth. By adopting techniques like reframing and gratitude and embracing a culture of growth, we can foster resilience and mental strength, ready to face whatever life throws our way.

Mental Toughness Exercises: Strengthening Your Inner Self

Imagine your mind as a muscle, capable of incredible feats, but only if you work it out regularly. Mental toughness is that muscle's strength, and just like you wouldn't expect a six-pack without some crunches, you can't expect a resilient mind without a little exercise. Let's start with visualization techniques for resilience. Picture this: a calm mountain lake, perfectly still, reflecting the colours of the sky. You close your eyes and imagine yourself there, feeling the cool breeze on your face. This isn't just wishful thinking; it's guided imagery, a technique that can reduce stress by transporting your mind to a place of peace. When you visualize positive outcomes, you train your brain to expect good results, laying the groundwork for handling life's curveballs with grace.

Focus and concentration drills are like push-ups for your brain. They hone your ability to zero in on tasks, shutting out distractions like a pro fencer parrying blows. Start with a simple exercise: pick an object, any object—a pencil, your coffee mug, or whatever's handy. Spend a couple of minutes observing every detail, the way the light hits it, its texture, the tiny imperfections. This drill enhances your focus, making it easier to concentrate on tasks when there's a cacophony of distractions. Think of it as tuning a radio to the right frequency; suddenly, everything becomes clear, and the noise fades away.

Now, let's talk about the benefits. These exercises offer more than just a mental workout. They boost emotional stability, helping you maintain control even when your world feels like it's spinning faster than a ceiling fan on high. Imagine facing a stressful situation at work—a tight deadline or a difficult client. Instead of panicking, you find yourself calm and collected, able to think clearly and act decisively. This control over stress and pressure is what mental toughness exercises aim to build. It's like having a mental toolkit at your disposal, ready to tackle any challenge that comes your way.

To get started, here's a step-by-step guide to guided imagery for stress reduction. Find a quiet spot where you won't be disturbed. Sit comfortably, close your eyes, and take a few deep breaths. Picture yourself in a relaxing place—a beach, a forest, wherever you find peace. Engage all your senses: feel the warmth of the sun, hear the gentle rustle of leaves, smell the fresh sea air. Spend a few minutes immersing yourself in this scene, letting your mind unwind. For mindfulness meditation, set aside five minutes each day. Sit quietly, focus on your breath, and let thoughts come and go without judgment. It's normal for your mind to wander—just gently bring your focus back to your breathing. These exercises are like mental pit stops, allowing you to recharge and refocus.

Consistency is key to building mental toughness. It's not about doing a marathon session once and calling it a day. Regular practice is what yields results. Establish a routine, maybe every morning or just before bed, whatever fits your schedule. Track your progress over time. Keep a journal, I keep saying journal, but you folks know by now it's whatever fits for you to note how these exercises affect your mood, stress levels, and ability to concentrate. You'll likely notice gradual improvements, and these small victories can be incredibly motivating. Think of it as planting seeds in a garden; with time and care, they'll grow into a lush landscape.

Building mental toughness is a journey of self-discovery. As you practice these exercises, you strengthen your mind and learn more about your inner self. You discover resilience you didn't know you had, and you develop a toolkit of strategies to handle whatever life throws at you. It's about finding that inner calm amidst the chaos, the eye of the storm where you can regroup and recharge. So, start small, be patient with yourself, and trust in the process. The rewards, both in terms of mental strength and self-awareness, are well worth the effort.

Finding Strength in Vulnerability: Embracing Your True Self

Ever felt like you're wearing a mask, smiling and nodding while inside, you're playing a different tune? That's the dance with vulnerability we often do, trying to maintain a brave face while hiding our true selves. But here's the kicker: vulnerability isn't a weakness; it's a hidden superpower. When you embrace vulnerability, you unlock a path to genuine strength and resilience. It's like peeling away the layers of an onion, revealing the raw, authentic core underneath. This connection between vulnerability and authenticity is profound. When you're true to yourself, you build an unshakeable foundation rooted in honesty and self-awareness. This authenticity fosters a deep understanding of who you are and allows others to see the real you, not just the façade. Overcoming the fear of vulnerability is like stepping into the spotlight without a script, trusting that your true self is enough. It's not about bearing all to everyone all the time, but about choosing to be honest in moments that matter, with people who matter.

Self-acceptance is the cornerstone of embracing vulnerability. It's about looking in the mirror and saying, "This is me, flaws and all, and that's okay." Practising self-love and compassion is your daily mantra, a reminder to treat yourself with the same kindness you'd offer a friend. It's giving yourself a mental hug, especially on the days when you feel like you're falling short. Sharing personal stories with trusted individuals can be transformative. It's like lifting a weight off your shoulders, allowing others to walk alongside you in your journey. When you open up to someone you trust, you invite connection and understanding, and you often find that your vulnerability is met with empathy, not judgment. These sharing moments foster intimacy, weaving a tapestry of relationships that support and nurture you.

Being authentic doesn't just enhance mental toughness; it's a lifeline to deeper connections and reduced anxiety. When you're genuine, you're not constantly juggling masks or pretending to be someone you're not. This authenticity builds trust, as people sense your sincerity and are drawn to your openness. It's like a magnet, attracting those who appreciate you for who you truly are. Genuine self-expression also alleviates anxiety. When you're not consumed by the fear of being found out, you can focus on what truly matters—being present, connecting with others, and embracing life's experiences. Authenticity liberates you from the constraints of superficiality, offering a sense of freedom and peace.

Let's explore some stories of individuals who found strength in their vulnerability. Consider Brené Brown, a researcher who turned her own struggles with vulnerability into a source of empowerment. By sharing her personal journey, she inspired millions to embrace their imperfections and live authentically. Her work highlights how vulnerability can be a catalyst for courage and connection. Then there's Maya Angelou, whose poetry and autobiographies laid bare her life's trials and triumphs. Her willingness to share her vulnerabilities created a powerful legacy of resilience and empowerment. These leaders teach us that embracing vulnerability is not about perfection; it's about being real, showing up as you are, and finding strength in that truth.

Testimonials from those who've embraced their true selves often reveal a profound sense of empowerment. One story might tell of someone who, after years of hiding their struggles with mental health, decided to speak openly about their experiences. This act of vulnerability brought personal healing and inspired others to seek help to share their own stories. Another might recount a CEO who, by admitting mistakes and sharing personal challenges, fostered a corporate culture of openness and trust. These examples illustrate that vulnerability, when embraced, can be a source of strength, transforming personal and professional relationships.

Embracing vulnerability is about stepping into the light, daring to be seen as you truly are. It's a journey toward self-acceptance and authenticity that enriches your life and the lives of those around you. As you navigate this path, remember that vulnerability is not a sign of weakness but a testament to your courage and resilience. In the next chapter, we'll explore how to integrate these lessons into your daily life, creating a harmony between your inner and outer worlds.

FOUR

Embracing Professional Help

Picture this: you're sitting at a coffee shop, your life scattered around you like the crumbs of a half-eaten croissant. You overhear a conversation where someone casually mentions their therapist, like they're talking about their favorite barista. "Therapy?" you wonder, as you sip your over-priced latte. "Is it like a mental spa day, or do they just sit there and nod while you spill your guts?" Well, let's lift the curtain on what therapy really is because it has the potential to be a game-changer for your mental health.

Therapy, or psychotherapy as the fancy folks at the National Institute of Mental Health call it, is like having a conversation with a purpose. It's not just chit-chat; it's a guided exploration of your thoughts, emotions, and behaviours with a licensed mental health professional. Think of it as a mental makeover where you get to identify and change troubling patterns. Therapy can be a solo adventure or a group affair, depending on what you find most comfortable. The goal? To relieve symptoms, enhance daily functioning, and improve your quality of life. It's like clearing out mental cobwebs and finding a clearer path forward.

You might be wondering about the types of therapy out there. It's a bit like choosing between different ice cream flavours, each with its own unique benefits. Cognitive Behavioral Therapy (CBT) is a popular choice, focusing on altering harmful thinking patterns—like swapping out those old, worn-out mental sneakers for shiny new ones. Then there's psychoanalysis, where you dive deep into your past to uncover hidden motivations, kind of like being a detective in your own life story. If mindfulness is more your speed, mindfulness-based therapy might be your jam, helping you stay grounded in the present moment.

The therapy process typically kicks off with an initial consultation, where you and your therapist get to know each other. It's like a first date without the awkward small talk. This session involves an assessment to understand your needs and challenges. From there, you'll work together to set goals and develop a treatment plan. Think of it as plotting a course on a map, with your therapist as the trusty guide. They're there to help you navigate the terrain, offering insights and strategies along the way.

Let's tackle some common misconceptions about therapy, shall we? First up, the myth that therapy is only for severe mental illness. That's like saying gyms are only for bodybuilders. Therapy is for everyone, whether you're dealing with a major crisis or just need a little mental tune-up. Another misconception is that therapists will judge or criticize you. In reality, therapists are trained to provide a non-judgmental space. They're like Switzerland—neutral and supportive, helping you explore your thoughts and feelings without fear of judgment.

The benefits of therapy are as varied as the people who seek it. Improved self-awareness and emotional regulation are often at the forefront. It's like getting a mental compass to help you understand your emotions and reactions. Therapy also enhances coping strategies for stress and anxiety, equipping you with tools to handle life's curveballs with greater ease. Imagine having a mental toolbox filled with strategies for those inevitable rough patches. It's about building resilience and finding a sense of balance and well-being.

Reflection Exercise: Consider Therapy

Take a moment to reflect on what you might want to gain from therapy. Is there a specific challenge or issue you'd like to address? What goals would you set for yourself? Jot down your thoughts in a journal or discuss them with a trusted friend. This exercise can help clarify your intentions and prepare you for the possibility of seeking professional help.

Therapy isn't a magic wand that makes problems disappear, but it's a powerful ally in the quest for mental wellness. When I first went to therapy, I believed it was like dropping off your laundry, and I'll be back to collect it at 5 pm; little did I realise just how tough it was. By demystifying the process and understanding its true purpose, you might find it's just the support you need. So, next time you're sipping that latte and pondering life's mysteries, consider whether therapy might be a step worth taking. Looking back, for me, it was, and I kissed many a frog before I found the right therapist for me.

Finding the Right Therapist for You

So, you've decided to give therapy a shot, and now you're staring at a list of therapists that's longer than your last grocery receipt. Where do you even begin? Start by defining what you're looking for. Are you hoping to tackle anxiety, work through past trauma, or perhaps just navigate life's curveballs a bit more smoothly? Identifying your personal therapy goals is like setting a GPS for your mental health road trip. Once you know what you're aiming for, you can narrow down your search to therapists who specialise in those areas. Each therapist has their own approach, like chefs with different cuisines. Some might offer a structured, goal-oriented method like Cognitive Behavioral Therapy, while others might engage you in deeper, exploratory sessions akin to psychoanalysis. It's about finding the flavour that suits your palate.

Next, dive into the nitty-gritty of researching therapists. Websites like psychologytoday.com or goodtherapy.org can be a goldmine of information. Each profile often details a therapist's credentials, areas of expertise, and therapeutic approach. Some might have videos or blogs to give you a taste of their style. Don't shy away from making a list of those who resonate with you. Consider factors like location and availability. Are they close enough for you to get to without turning it into a cross-country trek? Flexibility is another consideration; some therapists offer evening or weekend sessions, which can be a lifesaver if your schedule is as packed as a clown car. And let's not forget the cost. Therapy can range from £60 to £200 per session, but don't let sticker shock deter you. There are often sliding scale options or insurance coverage that can ease the financial burden. Sometimes, even employers will assist with costs, especially if you are off work, and it's seen as a cost to get you back to work.

The first meeting with a therapist can feel a bit like a blind date, minus the awkward small talk about the weather. You'll want to discuss their approach and how it aligns with your goals. Ask questions like, "What's your experience with clients facing similar challenges?" or "How do you typically structure your sessions?" This is your chance to set the tone for the relationship, an opportunity to discuss your expectations and any concerns you might have. It's also essential to gauge how comfortable you feel with them. Do they make you feel heard and understood, or are you counting the minutes until you can make a polite exit? Trust your gut—it's often the best judge in these situations.

As you continue with therapy, it's crucial to periodically evaluate the relationship. Is the therapist helping you make progress, or do you feel like you're spinning your wheels? Recognizing when things are going well is as important as spotting when they aren't. Therapy should feel like a safe space, not a chore. Be open to changing therapists if necessary. It's perfectly fine to switch if you feel that the fit isn't right. Think of it as trying on shoes—it might take a few pairs to find one that doesn't pinch. Remember, this is your mental health we're talking about, and you deserve the best support possible.

Making the Most of Your Therapy Sessions

Getting ready for a therapy session is a bit like preparing for a road trip. You wouldn't just hop in your car without a map or snacks, right? Therapy is your journey to self-discovery and healing, and preparation can make all the difference. Start by reflecting on recent challenges and experiences. This is your chance to think about what's been on your mind or what situations have been particularly tough. Maybe it's that argument with a friend who's been playing on a loop in your head, or the creeping anxiety that hits every Sunday night. Jot these down in a notebook or even on your phone. Identifying these areas gives you a launching point for each session.

Setting specific goals for each session can transform your therapy experience from a vague chat into a targeted exploration. Think about what you want to achieve. Is it clarity on a particular issue, or perhaps a strategy to tackle stress at work? Having clear objectives helps guide the conversation and ensures you're not just spinning your wheels. It's like having a checklist for the soul, ticking off boxes as you go. Share these goals with your therapist, so they know what you're aiming for. They're not mind readers, after all, and knowing your focus helps them tailor the session to your needs.

Once you're in the session, it's time to roll up your sleeves and dive in. Active participation is key. This isn't a spectator sport;

it's a collaborative effort between you and your therapist. Open communication with your therapist is crucial. Share your thoughts and feelings honestly, even if they're messy or uncomfortable. Remember, this is a safe space. It might feel daunting to explore difficult topics, but pushing through that discomfort is where the magic happens. It's like peeling back layers of an onion, revealing truths that might be tear-inducing but ultimately liberating.

Therapy doesn't stop when you leave the office. Implementing insights from sessions into your daily life is where real change takes root. It's all about practising new coping strategies and techniques you've discussed. Maybe it's using deep-breathing exercises when anxiety flares up, or challenging negative self-talk when it rears its ugly head. These tools aren't just for show; they're meant to be used. Keep a journal to track how these strategies play out. Jot down reflections and progress between sessions. It's a way to capture those "aha" moments and see how far you've come.

Monitoring progress is akin to checking your speedometer on a long drive. You want to know how fast you're going and if you're still on track. A therapy journal or progress log can be invaluable. Record your thoughts, feelings, and any significant changes you notice. It's like a personal diary of your mental health journey, where you can look back and see the shifts in your perspective. Discuss this progress regularly with your therapist. They can help you interpret patterns, celebrate victories, and adjust strategies if needed. Therapy is a dynamic process, and being attuned to your progress ensures you're moving in the right direction.

Therapy is a powerful tool for personal growth, but it requires engagement and effort. Being prepared, participating fully, and applying what you learn in your daily life are the keys to unlocking its potential. It's a commitment to yourself, a promise to seek understanding and healing.

When to Seek Professional Help: Recognising the Signs

There are days when life feels like you're trudging through molasses, and then there are days when it feels like you've been picked up by a tornado and spun around until you're dizzy. It's in these whirlwind moments that recognising the need for professional help becomes crucial. You see, we all have our off days, but when those days stretch into weeks or months of persistent sadness or anxiety, it's time to take notice. It's like that annoying car rattle that starts soft but gets louder over time—you can ignore it for a while, but eventually, it demands attention. If you find yourself struggling to get out of bed, losing interest in things you once loved, or constantly feeling on edge, these are your mind's check engine lights flashing. They're telling you something's not quite right.

Difficulty functioning in daily life is another telltale sign. Imagine trying to drive with the parking brake on—everything becomes a struggle. Tasks that used to be second nature suddenly feel insurmountable. You're late for work, missing deadlines, or maybe your relationships are starting to fray at the edges. It's as if you're walking through a fog, and no matter how hard you try, you can't seem to find your way out.

These aren't just rough patches; they're indicators that it might be time to reach out for a lifeline.

Getting help early can be a game-changer. Think of it like catching a cold before it turns into the flu. By seeking support sooner rather than later, you prevent mental health conditions from escalating into something more severe. Early intervention is like putting on a mental raincoat before the storm hits, equipping you with tools for better self-management. You're not just treating symptoms; you're building resilience and learning strategies to navigate future challenges with more ease. It's about gaining skills that help you weather life's inevitable ups and downs, turning potential crises into manageable hurdles.

Taking the first step to seek help can feel daunting, like standing at the edge of a pool, unsure whether to jump in. But it doesn't have to be a solo plunge. Start by reaching out to your GP for a referral. They can guide you toward the right resources- counselling, therapy, or support groups. Local mental health services or hotlines are also invaluable. They're like mental health GPS systems, pointing you in the right direction when you feel lost. Remember, reaching out for help isn't a sign of weakness; it's a step toward reclaiming control over your mental well-being.

Normalizing the process of seeking help is vital. It's time we shift the narrative from one of shame to one of strength. Sharing the success stories of those who've sought help can be powerful. Like the friend who finally saw a therapist and uncovered a wellspring of coping strategies that turned their life around. Or the colleague who joined a support group and found a community that helped them heal. These stories remind us that we're not alone and that seeking help is a courageous act. Therapy isn't just for "those people"; it's for anyone ready to make positive changes in their life. It's a sign of strength, a testament to your willingness to take charge and enhance your mental health.

Complementing Therapy: Resources and Tools

Imagine therapy as the main dish in a meal, but like any good meal, it's the sides that truly round out the experience. Support groups and community workshops are delicious extras that complement your therapy plate. They offer a chance to connect with others who might be navigating similar challenges, creating a sense of solidarity. In these settings, you can swap stories, share coping strategies, and maybe even find a few laughs along the way. These groups can be formal, like those organized by local mental health organizations, or informal, like a book club that discusses mental health topics. The beauty of these gatherings is that they remind you—you're not alone in this.

Now, let's mention the literary feast of self-help books and online courses (one of which you're currently reading). These resources can be powerful allies in your mental health journey. A well-chosen book can provide insights and strategies that resonate with your personal experiences, offering new perspectives that can enhance your therapy sessions. Online courses, on the other hand, often provide structured learning paths, complete with videos and exercises, to deepen your understanding of specific issues. Think of them as mini-therapy sessions you can revisit whenever you need a boost. The key is to pick resources that align with your goals, much like curating a music playlist that matches your mood.

When it comes to self-help tools, mindfulness apps for stress reduction are like having a pocket-sized therapist. Apps like Calm or Headspace offer guided meditations that can help you find your centre amidst the chaos. They're perfect for those moments when you need a break but can't quite make it to your therapist's office. Mood-tracking journals are another fantastic tool, allowing you to chart your emotional landscape over time. By noting how you feel each day, you can identify patterns and triggers, offering valuable insights you can bring to your therapy sessions. It's like being a detective in your own life story, piecing together clues to better understand your mental health.

Integrating these resources with your therapy isn't just a good idea; it's a game-changer. Imagine coordinating with your therapist to incorporate these tools into your treatment plan. It's like adding spices to a dish, enhancing the overall flavour. Setting goals that align with both therapy and self-help efforts can create a cohesive strategy for growth. For instance, if your therapy focuses on reducing anxiety, using a mindfulness app daily can reinforce the techniques you learn in sessions. Your therapist can offer guidance on which resources might be most beneficial, helping you tailor your approach to suit your needs.

The benefits of a holistic support system are immense. When therapy and complementary resources work in harmony, you gain a more profound understanding and management of your mental health. It's like having a toolbox full of diverse instruments, each playing a part in constructing a stronger foundation. This approach empowers you with greater autonomy in your personal growth, enabling you to take charge of your mental health journey. You become an active participant in your healing, rather than a passive observer. This empowerment fosters a sense of confidence and resilience, allowing you to face challenges with a newfound strength.

Overcoming Stigma: Break the Silence, Find Support

Picture this: you're contemplating whether to share with your friend that you've been seeing a therapist, but the words stick like peanut butter in your throat. You worry about what they'll think, the labels they might slap on you. This is stigma at work, a silent bully that creeps into our thoughts and builds barriers around seeking help. Stigma doesn't just discourage you from speaking up; it creates actual hurdles in accessing therapy and support. It's like putting up a "Do Not Enter" sign on the road to recovery. Many people internalize this stigma, leading to feelings of shame and self-judgment. You might find yourself wondering if asking for help means you've failed somehow, or that it's a sign of weakness. But let's be clear: needing support is as human as needing air.

To counter this, it's crucial to promote open conversations about mental health. Think of it as cracking open a window in a stuffy room, letting in fresh air and light. Sharing personal experiences with trusted friends or family can break the ice, opening the door to more honest discussions. It's not about broadcasting every detail but finding those you trust and allowing them to share in your journey. Participating in mental health awareness campaigns can also make a difference. Whether it's a local event or an online initiative, these platforms provide a megaphone for your voice, amplifying stories that inspire and educate others.

Community support plays a pivotal role in overcoming stigma. When you find allies in mental health advocacy, you're not just a lone voice in the wilderness; you're part of a chorus demanding change. Engaging with online support networks is another powerful strategy. They're like virtual villages where you can connect with like-minded individuals, share experiences, and find encouragement. These communities remind you that you're not alone, offering a space where stigma holds no power. It's about building a network that uplifts and empowers rather than isolates and shames.

Empowering yourself against stigma begins with self-acceptance and self-compassion. Practice seeing yourself through a lens of kindness, recognizing that your struggles don't define you. Self-acceptance is a bit like giving yourself a mental hug, acknowledging your worth and resilience. Educating yourself about mental health realities is equally important. Knowledge is a shield against misconceptions, arming you with facts that counter stigma. By understanding the nuances of mental health, you're better equipped to educate others, fostering an environment of understanding and support.

As we wrap up this chapter, remember that breaking the silence around mental health isn't just an act of defiance against stigma; it's a step toward healing. By sharing your truth and finding support, you pave the way for others to do the same. Next, we'll explore how to navigate the emotional challenges that life throws your way, ensuring you're not just surviving but thriving.

FIVE

Navigating Emotional Challenges

P icture this: You're at a bustling airport, surrounded by a cacophony of sounds—a baby crying, announcements blaring, people chattering—and then, suddenly, someone bumps into you, knocking your coffee onto your shirt. In that split second, an array of emotions rushes through you: surprise, irritation, and perhaps a bit of embarrassment. It's like the emotional version of a flash mob, each feeling clamoring for attention. This scenario illustrates perfectly the complex tapestry of our emotions. They're not just fleeting reactions; they're the colorful threads that weave through the fabric of our daily experiences, shaping how we perceive and interact with the world around us.

Let's start by unravelling the core emotions that form the foundation of our emotional spectrum. Think of them as the primary colours on an artist's palette—joy, sadness, anger, fear, and surprise. Each emotion serves a unique purpose, like a well-cast character in a play. Joy, for instance, is the charismatic lead, lighting up the stage and drawing us toward what brings us happiness and fulfilment. Sadness, often misunderstood, is the reflective poet, encouraging introspection and empathy. Anger, with its fiery energy, signals when boundaries have been crossed, urging us to take action. Fear, the cautious guardian, alerts us to potential danger, helping us stay safe. And surprise, the spontaneous jester, keeps life exciting, reminding us to expect the unexpected. These primary emotions, as identified by psychologists like Paul Ekman and Robert Plutchik, are universal, instinctual responses to stimuli, providing vital insights into our needs and desires (Source 1).

As we delve deeper, we encounter the intricate dance of complex emotions—those fascinating combinations and blends that arise from life's many experiences. Imagine emotions as a symphony, with primary emotions as the main notes and complex emotions as the harmonies that emerge from their interaction. A life event, like a career change, might stir a cocktail of excitement, anxiety, and hope, each emotion coloured by past successes and fears. These complex emotions are shaped by our personal beliefs, experiences, and current circumstances, adding depth to our emotional landscape. They remind us that our emotional world is as layered as a rich tapestry, each thread adding nuance and texture.

Understanding this complexity begins with cultivating emotional awareness. It's about tuning into the subtle shifts within us, much like a chef tasting a dish to balance flavours. Mindfulness becomes our trusted guide, helping us notice these shifts with curiosity rather than judgment. By pausing to observe our emotions, we create space to understand them more fully. It's like having a dialogue with your inner self, capturing the ebb and flow of feelings over time. You might jot down moments of joy or instances of frustration, noting what triggered them and how you responded. Over time, patterns emerge, offering insights into your emotional triggers and responses.

Interactive Element: Emotion Journal Prompt

As we explore our emotions, it's crucial to embrace them as natural and valid responses to life's events. Emotions, like the weather, are ever-changing, guiding us through the sunny days and stormy nights of our existence. Rather than labelling emotions as 'good' or 'bad,' consider them as signals, each with its own message to convey. By acknowledging emotions without judgment, we allow ourselves to experience them fully, reducing the burden of self-criticism. It's about giving ourselves permission to feel, to ride the wave of each emotion without fear of capsizing. In doing so, we foster a more compassionate relationship with ourselves, one where all emotions are welcomed and understood.

Anxiety Unpacked: Strategies for Calmness

Anxiety can be a bit like having an overzealous alarm system in your mind. You know, the kind that goes off when a leaf falls on your driveway. It's that feeling of unease, worry, or fear that creeps in, sometimes without a clear cause, leaving you on edge. While stress tends to have an external trigger—think deadlines or traffic jams—anxiety often lingers, like a shadow that follows you even when the stressor is gone.

Symptoms can vary from a racing heart to a mind that jumps around like a squirrel on caffeine. You might feel tense or restless, find it difficult to concentrate, or even experience physical symptoms like headaches or a knotted stomach. Unlike stress, which ebbs and flows with life's demands, anxiety can stick around, making everyday tasks feel overwhelming.

To manage anxiety, it helps to know what sets it off. Triggers can be as varied as the colours in a box of crayons. Some might be situational, like the thought of speaking in public, which can send your heart into a drum solo. Internal triggers are sneakier, often stemming from negative self-talk or perfectionist tendencies. It's that little voice that whispers, "What if I mess up?" or "I must get this perfect." Identifying these triggers is like shining a flashlight into a dark room, helping you understand what's fueling your anxiety. Once you know your triggers, you can start to develop strategies to manage them effectively.

When anxiety strikes, calming techniques can be your best friend. Deep breathing is a classic, and for good reason. It's like hitting the reset button on your nervous system. Try this: inhale deeply through your nose for a count of four, hold for four, then exhale through your mouth for another count of four. Repeat until your heartbeat slows, and your mind starts to quiet. Grounding techniques can also help pull you back to the present. A simple exercise is to engage your senses— notice five things you can see, four you can touch, three you can hear, two you can smell, and one you can taste. This practice anchors you in the here and now, gently redirecting your focus from the whirlpool of anxious thoughts.

For long-term anxiety management, building a routine is key. Regular exercise is like a release valve for pent-up stress, flooding your body with feel-good chemicals that boost your mood. Whether it's a brisk walk, a dance class, or hitting the gym, moving your body helps burn off the excess energy that anxiety brings. Daily meditation is another powerful tool. It's like training your mind to find calm amidst chaos. Even just a few minutes of sitting quietly and focusing on your breath can build resilience over time. Cognitive-behavioural techniques are also worth exploring. They help rewire negative thought patterns, turning that critical inner voice into a supportive coach. Think of these strategies as a toolkit; each one offers a different way to tackle anxiety, helping you feel more grounded and in control.

Anxiety might feel like a constant companion, but with the right tools and strategies, you can turn down its volume. It's about finding what works for you, planning, and practising these skills regularly. Like learning a new skill, it takes time and patience, but the freedom and peace it brings are well worth the effort.

Battling the Blues: Overcoming Everyday Sadness

We all have those days when life feels like an old pair of socks —worn out and just a bit saggy. You know, the kind of day when everything seems to be painted in shades of grey, and even the simplest tasks feel like wading through custard. This is what I mean by everyday sadness, a fleeting guest that visits unannounced but doesn't overstay its welcome. It's different from clinical depression, which hangs around like an unwanted relative, casting a long shadow over your life. Everyday sadness is often situational, sparked by a rough day at work or a spat with a friend, and tends to lift once the clouds have cleared. It's transient and can usually be managed with a few simple tweaks to your routine. Understanding this distinction is crucial, as it empowers you to address these feelings without the weight of a clinical diagnosis.

When that melancholy mood takes hold, finding ways to shake things up can be a game-changer. Dive into creative activities—think of it as therapy without the couch. Painting, drawing, or even doodling can help channel those blues into something tangible and, dare I say, beautiful. It's not about creating a masterpiece for the Louvre; it's about expressing emotions in a way that words can't quite capture. And if art supplies aren't your thing, try plugging into some uplifting tunes or a feel-good podcast. Music has this magical ability to speak directly to our souls, lifting spirits when words fail. Whether it's the soothing strum of a guitar or a podcast filled with laughter and inspiration, these auditory escapes can act as a balm for a weary heart.

Cultivating a positive mindset doesn't mean plastering on a fake smile and calling it a day. It's about training your brain to spot the silver linings, even when they're buried under a pile of laundry. Practising gratitude is a powerful way to shift your perspective. Try thinking of three things you're thankful for each night. It could be as simple as a cup of warm tea or the fact that your favourite song came on the radio. Over time, this practice can transform your outlook, focusing on what's right rather than what's wrong. Reframing negative thoughts can also help. When you catch yourself spiralling into a pit of despair, pause and challenge those thoughts. Instead of thinking, "I'm a failure," ask yourself, "What can I learn from this experience?" It's about turning those negative narratives into opportunities for growth and understanding.

When life hands you lemons, sometimes you just need to step outside and breathe in the fresh air. Spending time in nature is one of those underrated remedies that can work wonders for your mood. Whether it's a stroll through a park or a hike in the woods, being surrounded by greenery can help reset your mind, offering a moment of peace amidst the chaos. And if you're looking to boost your spirits while giving back, consider volunteering. Helping others can provide a sense of purpose and fulfilment, pulling you out of your head and into the community. Whether it's serving meals at a shelter or spending time with animals at a rescue, these acts of kindness not only lift others but can elevate your own mood, too.

Everyday sadness is an inevitable part of the human experience, but it doesn't have to define your day. By recognizing its transient nature and implementing these coping mechanisms, you can navigate those grey days with resilience, emerging stronger and more attuned to the beauty that life has to offer.

Handling Emotional Triggers: Techniques for Stability

Picture this: you're at a family gathering, minding your own business, when a relative drops a comment that hits you like a ton of bricks. Instantly, you're flooded with emotions, reacting before you even realise what's happening. That, my friend, is an emotional trigger in action. These triggers are like invisible buttons that, when pressed, can send us spiralling into a whirlwind of feelings. They often stem from experiences, like memories lurking just below the surface, waiting for the right moment to resurface. A snide remark might remind you of childhood teasing, or a chaotic environment could echo past times when you felt out of control. Recognising these triggers is the first step in diffusing their power. It's about understanding the connection between the past and the present and acknowledging how certain people or situations cause these strong reactions.

Once you've identified your triggers, it's time to arm yourself with coping strategies. Think of it as building your personal toolkit for emotional regulation. First up, assertive communication. When a trigger is pulled, instead of shutting down or exploding, practice expressing your feelings calmly and clearly. It's like finding the volume control on your emotions, allowing you to respond rather than react. For instance, if a friend's comment stings, try saying, "When you said that, it made me feel undervalued. Can we talk about it?" This opens a dialogue, giving you both a chance to understand each other better. Assertive communication isn't about confrontation; it's about expressing yourself honestly while respecting the other person's viewpoint. It's a skill that takes practice, but it can transform how you handle emotionally charged situations.

Mindful reactions are another powerful tool in your toolkit. Imagine you're in the middle of a heated discussion, and you feel the familiar rush of adrenaline. Before reacting, take a moment to pause and breathe. A few deep breaths can create a buffer between stimulus and response, allowing you precious seconds to regain composure. This pause allows you to observe your emotions non-judgmentally, like a scientist studying a specimen without bias. Instead of labelling your feelings as 'bad' or 'wrong,' accept them as natural responses to the situation. This practice of mindful observation helps you respond with clarity and intention rather than being swept away by the tide of emotion.

Building emotional resilience is about creating a support system that buffers you against the impact of triggers. Surround yourself with friends who lift you up, those who understand and accept you as you are. A strong network is like a safety net, catching you when you feel like you're free-falling. Regularly practising relaxation techniques is equally important. Whether it's yoga, meditation, or simply taking a few moments each day to unwind, these practices help reset your nervous system, making you more resilient to stress. They're like mental workouts, strengthening your ability to remain calm under pressure.

Handling emotional triggers isn't about avoiding them alto-gether—that's like trying to dodge raindrops in a storm. Instead, it's about equipping yourself with the skills and support to navigate through them with grace and confidence. By identifying triggers, developing coping strategies, prac-tising mindfulness, and building resilience, you can transform how you respond to the world around you. You're not at the mercy of your triggers; you have the power to manage them.

Mastering Emotional Intelligence: The Key to Better
Relationships

Emotional Intelligence, or EI, is like having a secret weapon
in your back pocket—it's the ability to navigate the emotional
landscape with grace and skill. When we talk about EI, we're
diving into a world where self-awareness, self-regulation,
empathy, and social skills reign supreme. Imagine being able
to recognize your own emotions and manage them effectively,
like mastering the controls of a flight simulator. This self-
awareness is the cornerstone of EI, allowing you to understand your emotional triggers and responses. It's the reason
you can catch yourself before snapping at a friend over something trivial. Self-regulation, on the other hand, is like having
a personal emotional thermostat, adjusting your responses to
maintain balance. Whether you're simmering in traffic or
dealing with a challenging coworker, self-regulation keeps
you from boiling over. Empathy, another crucial component,
is the superpower that lets you step into someone else's shoes
and truly understand how they feel. It's what transforms a
good listener into a great friend or partner. And social skills?
They're the polished dance moves that help you glide through
conversations and interactions, fostering connections and
resolving conflicts with finesse. Together, these elements of
EI don't just boost your personal life; they're game-changers
in the professional arena, too, enhancing teamwork, leader-
ship, and overall success.

To boost self-awareness, reflective journaling becomes your
trusty sidekick. Picture this: at the end of the day, you sit
down with a cup of tea, pen in hand, and jot down your

thoughts and feelings. What made you smile today? What moments left you feeling off-kilter? By exploring these questions, you create a dialogue with yourself, uncovering patterns and gaining insights into your emotional world. It's like having a heart-to-heart with your inner self, peeling back the layers to reveal what truly matters. Seeking feedback from trusted friends or colleagues is another avenue. They offer perspectives you might not have considered, gently pointing out blind spots or areas for growth. It's like having a personal coach cheering you on, helping you fine-tune your emotional radar.

Enhancing empathy is an art worth mastering. Start with active listening exercises. Imagine having a conversation where you focus solely on the speaker, tuning out distractions and really hearing what they're saying. It's not just about waiting for your turn to speak; it's about giving the other person the gift of your undivided attention. This simple act strengthens bonds and builds trust, showing that you value their perspective. Role-playing is another tool to deepen empathy. Whether it's reenacting a recent disagreement or stepping into a fictional scenario, role-playing allows you to see the world through different eyes. It's like a mental rehearsal, preparing you to respond with understanding and compassion in real-life situations.

Applying EI in relationships is where the magic truly happens. Open and honest communication is the cornerstone of any strong relationship. It's about speaking your truth and creating a space where others feel safe to do the same. Imagine a disagreement where, instead of raising voices, both parties express their feelings and listen with an open heart.

This approach transforms conflict into an opportunity for growth, where empathy and understanding lead the way. Resolving conflicts with empathy involves recognizing the emotions at play and striving to understand the other person's viewpoint. It's about finding common ground and working together to reach a resolution rather than viewing each other as adversaries. In this way, EI becomes a bridge, connecting hearts and minds and paving the way for deeper, more meaningful relationships.

Emotional Intelligence isn't just a buzzword; it's a life skill that enriches every interaction and relationship. By enhancing self-awareness, improving empathy, and applying these principles in our connections with others, we create a tapestry of understanding and support that uplifts us all. Sounds spectacular. Unsurprisingly, I'm still working on this one.

Cultivating Empathy: Connecting with Others

Imagine you're at a party, and someone spills a drink on themselves. Sympathy might have you offering a tissue with a light chuckle. Empathy, though, has you feeling the heat of their embarrassment and offering a kind word, making them feel less alone at that moment. Empathy is the ability to truly understand and share the feelings of another, while sympathy is more about acknowledging someone else's misfortune without deeply connecting to their emotional experience. This distinction is crucial because empathy builds bridges between people, forging connections that are both profound and enduring. When we engage empathically, we create a shared emotional landscape, deepening our social bonds and fostering a sense of belonging and trust. It's like having a backstage pass to someone's inner world, where you can appreciate their highs and lows and support them authentically.

Developing empathic listening skills is like tuning into a radio station that's broadcasting someone else's life story. It starts with maintaining eye contact, which signals your genuine interest and presence. This isn't about staring intently but about engaging with an open, friendly gaze that says, "I'm here, and I'm listening." Full attention is crucial—put the phone down, turn off the TV, and focus on the speaker. This undivided attention is a gift in our distraction-filled world, making the speaker feel valued and heard. Reflecting back on what the speaker has said is another key component. It involves paraphrasing or summarizing their words to ensure you've understood their message correctly. It's like holding up a mirror to their emotions, showing them you're not only listening but truly comprehending their experience. This validation can be incredibly powerful, affirming their feelings and strengthening your connection.

Perspective-taking exercises can transform how we relate to others, broadening our understanding of diverse experiences. Imagine putting on someone else's shoes and walking a mile in them—what would their journey feel like? This mental exercise encourages you to imagine yourself in another's situation, considering how their history, challenges, or dreams shape their perspective. Participating in group discussions that explore diverse viewpoints can also enhance this skill. By engaging with people from different backgrounds, you expose yourself to various perspectives, challenging your assumptions and enriching your worldview. This practice not only fosters empathy but enhances your capacity to relate to others on a deeper level, cultivating a more inclusive and compassionate mindset.

Fostering a culture of empathy within communities can have a ripple effect, transforming interactions and relationships. Volunteering for community service is a tangible way to practice empathy, putting yourself in situations where you can see the world through another's eyes. Whether serving meals at a shelter, tutoring children, participating in environmental clean-ups or being a marshal at the local park run, volunteering connects you with people outside your usual circle, opening your heart to their joys and struggles. Empathy-building workshops offer another avenue for growth. These workshops, often facilitated by experts, provide tools and strategies to enhance empathy, focusing on active listening, perspective-taking, and emotional intelligence. They create safe spaces for participants to explore emotions and experiences, leading to deeper understanding and mutual respect.

Summarising the role of empathy in our lives, it's clear that this skill is not just about improving personal relationships but about building a more connected and compassionate world. Empathy allows us to bridge the gaps between us, fostering deeper understanding and support. As we hone our empathic skills, we not only enhance our relationships but contribute to a culture of kindness and respect. In the next chapter, we'll explore how these emotional connections can be nurtured and maintained, ensuring they remain strong and resilient amidst life's challenges.

SIX

Enhancing Personal Growth and Mindset

There I was, about to make my third attempt at assembling a flat-pack desk, when it hit me: this was my life in a nutshell. You know, the kind of situation where you start with all the enthusiasm in the world, only to end up surrounded by a sea of screws and incomprehensible instructions. Life has a funny way of throwing challenges at us, much like those cryptic assembly manuals that seem designed to humble even the most seasoned DIY enthusiast. The difference between those who thrive and those who merely survive often boils down to mindset. Specifically, a growth mindset—a concept as crucial as a trusty Allen wrench in the toolbox of life.

A growth mindset is the belief that abilities and intelligence can be developed with effort and learning. It's like seeing life as a series of puzzles to solve, rather than a fixed path. In contrast, a fixed mindset is akin to believing you're born with a certain number of puzzle pieces, and that's all you'll ever have. These two mindsets shape how you approach challenges. With a growth mindset, challenges become opportunities for growth rather than threats to your self-esteem. It's like seeing a new puzzle piece and thinking, "Great, where does this fit?" instead of, "Oh no, another piece to deal with."

The benefits of a growth mindset are as vast as the ocean, rippling out to enhance mental health and resilience. When you adopt this mindset, motivation and perseverance come naturally. It's like having a personal cheerleader in your head, encouraging you to keep going even when the going gets tough. Criticism transforms from a scary monster under the bed into a friendly guide showing you where to improve. You learn to see feedback as a tool for growth, not as a reflection of your worth. It's like finally realizing that constructive feedback is the GPS that helps you navigate life's winding roads more effectively.

Cultivating a growth mindset doesn't happen overnight; it's more of a journey than a destination. Start by seeking feedback and learning from others. Think of it as collecting pearls of wisdom from those who have walked the path before you. Embrace failure as a learning opportunity. It's not about glorifying failure but understanding that each misstep is a stepping stone to success. Remember, even the best chefs burn a few dishes before perfecting their recipes. It's about viewing each setback as a chance to tweak your approach and try again, armed with new insights and determination.

Real-life examples abound, showcasing the transformative power of a growth mindset. Consider J.K. Rowling, who faced multiple rejections before finally publishing the Harry Potter series. Her story is a testament to the power of persistence and the belief that each rejection was simply a redirection toward the right path. Or take the story of Thomas Edison, who viewed his thousands of failed attempts at creating the lightbulb as essential experiments leading to eventual success. These individuals exemplify how embracing a growth mindset can lead to breakthroughs that not only change their lives but also impact the world.

The journey to developing a growth mindset is ongoing, filled with twists and turns that challenge and inspire us. It's about opening yourself up to possibilities, learning from every experience, and understanding that growth is a continuous process. With each step forward, you build resilience, confidence, and a deeper understanding of your potential. It's about embracing the mindset of a lifelong learner, constantly evolving and growing, ready to tackle whatever life throws your way with grit and grace.

Goal Setting for Personal Growth: Making It Happen

Goal setting might seem like a no-brainer, but it's the secret sauce that keeps everything in life from feeling like you're just running in circles. It's the GPS that provides direction and purpose, steering you away from those moments when you're standing in the cereal aisle, overwhelmed by the choices, with no idea which box to grab. Goals give you something to aim for, a beacon in the fog of everyday chaos. They encourage accountability, keeping you focused and on track. Without goals, it's easy to drift through life like a leaf in the wind. But with them, you can chart a course and navigate through challenges with confidence.

Enter SMART goals, the superhero of goal-setting techniques. SMART stands for Specific, Measurable, Achievable, Relevant, and Time-bound. Imagine you're trying to build a LEGO castle without a picture on the box. That's what setting vague goals feels like. SMART goals make sure you have a clear picture of what you're working towards. They turn the abstract into the concrete, breaking your aspirations into manageable steps. By setting specific targets, you know exactly what you're aiming for. Measuring progress becomes straightforward, like ticking off items on a grocery list. Achievable goals ensure you're not reaching for the stars without a ladder, keeping your ambitions grounded in reality. Relevant goals align with your values, ensuring you're not chasing someone else's dreams. And setting timelines creates a sense of urgency, preventing procrastination from sneaking in.

Now, how do you actually set these goals? One method is to create a vision board. Cut out images and words that resonate with your goals and paste them onto a board. It's like crafting a visual roadmap to your future. Place it somewhere you'll see often, a daily reminder of where you're headed. Regular goal reviews are also crucial. Set aside time to evaluate your progress and make adjustments. Maybe your original timeline was too ambitious, or perhaps life threw you a curveball. Adjusting goals doesn't mean failure; it's about being flexible and responsive to change. Think of it like adjusting the sails on a boat to catch the wind more effectively.

Persistence and patience are your best friends when it comes to achieving goals. It's easy to feel disheartened when things don't go as planned, but remember, progress is still progress, no matter how small. Celebrate these small victories along the way. Did you finally manage to stick to your workout routine for a month? Give yourself a pat on the back—or maybe a slice of cake. Celebrating progress keeps motivation high and reminds you of how far you've come. Understanding that setbacks are part of the process is crucial. They're not road-blocks; they're detours that offer new perspectives. Embrace them, learn from them, and keep moving forward.

Creating a checklist of goals or even a success journal can help track achievements and setbacks. Write down what worked, what didn't, and what you learned. This practice not only keeps you organized but also serves as a motivational tool. When you see your progress laid out, it's easier to stay committed to your long-term vision. Remember, achieving goals isn't about sprinting to the finish line; it's a marathon that requires endurance and resilience. Stay focused, stay patient, and let your goals guide you to where you want to be.

The Art of Reflection: Learning from Your Experiences

Imagine your mind as a cluttered attic. It's full of old memories, forgotten dreams, and dusty regrets. The attic needs tidying, and reflection is your broom. By reflecting, you sift through the clutter, finding hidden gems and tossing out the junk. Reflection isn't just about dwelling on the past; it's about understanding it to shape your future. When you reflect, you identify your strengths and acknowledge areas for improvement. It's like holding a mirror up to your life, seeing the good, the bad, and the ugly with clarity. This self-awareness fuels personal growth, helping you make informed decisions and avoid past mistakes. By understanding what worked and what didn't, you can tailor your actions to better align with your goals and values.

To incorporate reflection into daily life, consider journaling. It's not just for moody teenagers. Journaling is a powerful exercise for self-discovery, capturing your thoughts and emotions on paper. It's like having a conversation with yourself, where you can be brutally honest without fear of judgment. Start with simple prompts like, "What am I grateful for today?" or "What challenged me this week?" These questions encourage you to delve deeper into your experiences, revealing patterns and insights that might otherwise go unnoticed. Another reflective practice is mind mapping. It's a visual technique that helps organize experiences and thoughts. Start with a central idea or event, then branch out with related thoughts, emotions, and lessons learned. It's like creating a roadmap of your mind, highlighting connections and revealing paths forward.

For those seeking deeper reflection, guided meditation is an excellent method for introspection. In a quiet space, close your eyes and focus on your breath. Let your thoughts come and go, observing them without judgment. This practice helps you tune into your inner voice, offering clarity and perspective. Reflective conversations with mentors can also be invaluable. These discussions provide an external viewpoint, offering insights you might overlook. Mentors can challenge your assumptions and offer wisdom drawn from their experiences. It's like having a sounding board that amplifies your understanding, helping you glean more from your reflections.

Regular reflection should become a habit, like brushing your teeth or checking your phone. Schedule reflection sessions in your week, setting aside time to pause and think. It could be a quiet Sunday afternoon with a cup of tea, or a weekday evening walk. Use reflection prompts to guide your thinking, such as "What did I learn today?" or "How did I handle conflict this week?" These prompts act as anchors, focusing your mind and encouraging deeper contemplation. Through regular reflection, you cultivate a habit of introspection, fostering a deeper connection with yourself.

Interactive Element: Reflection Prompts for Self-Discovery

- What is one thing I did well today, and how can I build on it?
- What didn't go as planned, and what can I learn from it?
- How did I feel in challenging situations, and what does that reveal about me?
- Who inspired me recently, and why?
- How can I apply what I learned today to future situations?

Reflection is like a personal growth toolkit, filled with insights waiting to be uncovered. It's a way to pause, step back, and view your life with fresh eyes. Through reflection, you gain a clearer understanding of who you are and who you want to be.

Embracing Change: The Path to Transformation

Change. It's that tricky little gremlin that sneaks into our lives when we least expect it, shaking things up like a snow globe. But here's the kicker: change is also the catalyst for growth. Without it, we'd all be stuck in the same spot, like a scratched record playing the same tune over and over. Change pushes us forward, forcing us to adapt and evolve. It's the spice of life, adding flavor and variety to our otherwise predictable routines. Whether it's a career shift, a new relationship, or even just trying a different route to work, change keeps us on our toes, reminding us that life is anything but static. Embracing change is like dancing in the rain rather than waiting for the storm to pass. It's about recognizing that change is inevitable, a constant companion in our journey through life.

Yet, despite knowing change is coming, it often brings with it a suitcase full of fears. The unknown can be daunting, like stepping into a pitch-black room with no clue what's inside. It's human nature to crave certainty and control, to want to know what tomorrow holds. The fear of losing that control can be paralyzing, causing us to cling to the familiar even when it no longer serves us. But, here's the thing about control: it's often just an illusion. Life rarely follows the script we write, and that's okay. It's in these moments of uncertainty that we find our strength and resilience. Overcoming the fear of change requires a shift in perspective, seeing it not as a threat but as an opportunity to break free from the confines of our comfort zones.

So, how do you embrace change without losing your marbles? Start by developing adaptability and flexibility. Think of yourself as a tree in a storm, bending with the wind rather than snapping under its force. Being adaptable means staying open to new ideas and perspectives, willing to adjust your sails when the wind changes direction. Practicing acceptance is also key. It's about letting go of the need to control every outcome, trusting that things will unfold as they should, even if it's not according to your original plan. Letting go can feel like unclenching a fist that's been tightly closed for too long, allowing yourself to breathe and move with more freedom.

Change isn't just a source of anxiety; it's a gateway to new experiences and perspectives. Each change brings with it a plethora of opportunities for personal and professional growth. Maybe it's a new career path that reignites your passion or a chance encounter that leads to a lifelong friendship. Change broadens your horizons, introducing you to new ways of thinking and living. It's like adding new colours to your palette, enriching the tapestry of your life. Embracing change opens doors you never knew existed, leading to a more fulfilling and dynamic existence.

In the end, change is neither good nor bad—it's simply part of life. It's how you respond to it that makes all the difference. By welcoming change with open arms, you create space for growth and transformation, allowing yourself to evolve and thrive. So, when change comes knocking, greet it with curiosity and courage, ready to explore the new paths it presents.

Overcoming Resistance: Breaking Free from Comfort Zones

Picture the moment when you're standing at the edge of a diving board, toes curled over the edge, heart pounding like a drum. That's resistance—a potent mix of fear and hesitation keeping you from diving into the unknown. This resistance is the invisible barrier that holds us back from growth, whispering all the reasons to stay put. It's closely tied to our comfort zones, those cosy bubbles where everything feels safe and predictable. While comfort zones provide a sense of security, they can also become prisons of complacency, lulling us into a false sense of satisfaction. But here's the catch: staying in these zones means missing out on the thrill of discovery and the opportunities that come with stepping beyond the familiar.

The impact of lingering in comfort zones is like watching your favourite TV show on a loop—there's comfort in the familiar, but eventually, it gets monotonous. When you choose to stay within these boundaries, you risk stagnation. Opportunities for learning and development slip through your fingers like sand, leaving you with the same old patterns and experiences. It's akin to reading the same book repeatedly, where the plot never changes, and the characters never evolve. Over time, this stagnation can lead to a lack of progress, both personally and professionally. You might wake up one day feeling stuck in a rut, wondering why things aren't moving forward when in reality, the key lies in your willing-ness to step outside that well-worn path.

Breaking free from the grip of resistance requires courage and a few strategic moves. Start by gradually exposing yourself to new experiences, much like dipping your toes in the water before diving in. Begin with small, manageable challenges that push you slightly beyond your comfort zone. It could be trying a new hobby, speaking up in a meeting, or exploring a different route to work. These incremental steps build confi-dence, easing the transition from the familiar to the unknown. Think of it as a workout for your resilience muscle —the more you practice, the stronger it becomes.

Embracing discomfort is where the magic happens. It's about rewiring your brain to see discomfort not as a threat but as a sign of growth. When you find yourself in a new situation, take a moment to breathe and acknowledge the unease. Instead of retreating, lean into it, recognizing that these moments of discomfort are where true growth occurs. Practising resilience in such situations is like learning to dance in the rain, finding grace and strength amidst the chaos. Over time, your tolerance for discomfort increases, allowing you to tackle bigger challenges with confidence and perseverance.

Visualize discomfort as a ladder leading to new heights. Each rung might feel shaky at first, but with each step you take, you gain a broader perspective of what you're capable of achieving. It's a journey of self-discovery, where you learn to trust yourself and your ability to adapt. The thrill of new experiences far outweighs the temporary discomfort, enriching your life with fresh perspectives and insights. So, take a deep breath, gather your courage, and take that leap off the diving board—you might just find that the water is more refreshing than you ever imagined.

Celebrating Small Wins: Motivation for Continued Growth

Picture this: You've just put in a solid hour at the gym, and you're feeling like a superhero. Sure, you didn't lift a car or run a marathon, but you showed up. That's a victory right there—a small win worth celebrating. Small achievements are the unsung heroes of personal growth, boosting motivation and morale like a shot of espresso on a sleepy morning. They reinforce positive behaviour and habits, creating a ripple effect that builds momentum toward larger goals. It's like laying bricks for a house; each small victory adds strength and stability to your foundation. When you acknowledge these wins, you're telling yourself, "Hey, I'm doing something right here." This reinforcement encourages you to keep moving forward, turning small steps into big strides over time.

Acknowledging your achievements doesn't have to be a grand affair. Sometimes, the simplest gestures carry the most weight. Consider keeping a success journal—a dedicated notebook where you jot down your daily victories, big or small. It's like a personal treasure chest filled with moments that remind you of your potential. Flip through it whenever you need a boost, and watch your confidence soar. Another way to celebrate is by rewarding yourself. Maybe it's a new book, a favourite meal, or just an afternoon off to do absolutely nothing. Whatever it is, make sure it feels like a genuine treat, a nod to your hard work and perseverance. These rewards act as powerful motivators, reinforcing the notion that effort leads to positive outcomes.

The psychological benefits of celebrating small wins are profound. Each acknowledgement increases your confidence and self-esteem, providing a sense of achievement that propels you forward. It's like fueling a fire; every little win adds another log, keeping the flames of motivation burning brightly. When you celebrate progress, no matter how incremental, you enhance your sense of progress. It's a reminder that you're moving in the right direction, even if the finish line isn't yet in sight. This heightened awareness of your achievements fosters a positive mindset, one that's resilient and ready to tackle future challenges with renewed vigour.

Creating a culture of celebration isn't just about individual recognition; it's about fostering an environment that values all achievements. Share your successes with friends and family, inviting them to celebrate alongside you. It's like popping a bottle of champagne; everything tastes better when shared with others. These communal celebrations build a support network that encourages continued growth. They create a space where everyone's achievements are acknowledged, no matter how small. Consider establishing communal recognition practices, like a weekly team meeting where everyone shares a win. These practices cultivate a sense of belonging and mutual support, reinforcing the idea that growth is a shared journey.

Celebrating small wins isn't just a feel-good exercise; it's a strategic approach to maintaining momentum and motivation. By recognizing these achievements, you build a resilient mindset that embraces progress as a continuous path rather than a final destination. It's about appreciating the journey and understanding that each step, no matter how small, brings you closer to your goals. As you embrace this practice, you'll find that the journey is enriched, the challenges more manageable, and the triumphs all the more rewarding. It's a reminder that growth is a process, one that's best savoured and celebrated along the way.

SEVEN

Balancing Life and Mental Health

E ver felt like you're juggling flaming torches while riding a unicycle on a tightrope? That's how life feels when work and personal demands clash. Work-life balance might sound like a myth, whispered about in coffee shops and motivational posters, but it's more attainable than you think. It's the delicate art of balancing professional responsibilities with personal life without feeling like you're constantly teetering on the edge. For your mental health, it's as vital as oxygen. When you master this balance, you create a buffer against stress, prevent burnout, and allow yourself to recharge, which is essential for maintaining your overall well-being. Without it, you're like a phone running on power-saving mode, barely getting through the day before crashing.

Balancing responsibilities doesn't mean giving equal time to work and play every day. It's about finding an equilibrium that suits your life's unique rhythm. It's recognizing that some days work will demand more, and other days, personal life takes the front seat. The goal is to avoid chronic imbalance where work consistently overshadows personal time, leading to fatigue and a parade of mental health challenges like anxiety or depression. Common challenges in achieving this balance include society's hustle culture and the internal pressures we place on ourselves to be everything to everyone. It's easy to fall into the trap of thinking we need to be the perfect employee, parent, friend, and partner all at once, but that's a surefire recipe for stress.

So, how do you achieve this elusive balance without tearing your hair out? Start with setting priorities. It's like packing a suitcase; not everything will fit, so choose what's essential. Identify your core responsibilities and values, and let them guide your decisions. If family time is crucial, make it non-negotiable in your schedule. Managing time effectively is another game-changer. Use tools like planners or digital calendars to block out time for work tasks and personal activities. This visual representation of your day can help you stick to your priorities and avoid overcommitting. Establishing clear boundaries between work and home is key—think of it as drawing a line in the sand where work ends and personal life begins. Whether it's shutting down your laptop by 6 PM or resisting the urge to check emails on weekends, these boundaries protect your mental space.

In today's world, flexible working options have become more common, and they offer a lifeline to those seeking balance. Telecommuting and remote work have their perks. They can save you from the hassle of commuting, giving you back precious hours that can be spent on personal pursuits. Adjusting work hours to fit your needs is like having a tailor-made suit; it just fits better. Maybe you're a morning person who thrives before the sun rises, or perhaps you hit your stride in the afternoon. Flexible work arrangements can allow you to align your work schedule with your natural rhythm, boosting productivity and satisfaction.

The benefits of maintaining work-life balance ripple through every aspect of your life. Reduced stress and burnout are immediate perks, as you're no longer running on fumes. You'll likely notice an improvement in personal relationships, too. When you're not constantly preoccupied with work, you can be present with loved ones, fostering deeper connections and happiness. Satisfaction grows as you create a life that aligns with your values and goals, leading to a more fulfilling existence. It's like finding the sweet spot on a seesaw, where everything feels just right.

Interactive Element: Personal Balance Check-in

Take a moment to reflect on your current work-life balance. On a scale from 1 to 10, how balanced do you feel? What are the areas where you feel most out of sync? Write down three small changes you can make to improve your balance this week. Maybe it's leaving work on time, setting up a family dinner night, or simply taking a walk during lunch. Revisit your check-in weekly to track progress and make adjustments as needed.

Mindful Productivity: Achieving More with Less Stress

Ever notice how life can feel like a never-ending game of Tetris, with tasks stacking up faster than you can clear them? That's where mindful productivity comes in. It's not about cramming more into your day but focusing on what truly matters. Imagine savouring a gourmet meal instead of wolfing down fast food. Mindful productivity is about quality over quantity in what you do. It's about being fully present and focused on each task rather than juggling so many plates that you end up with scrambled eggs on the floor. This approach reduces stress, as you're not constantly racing against the clock, and allows you to enjoy your work rather than just endure it.

So, how do you make your workday more like a zen garden and less like a battlefield? Start with time-blocking and single-tasking. Time-blocking is like setting up dedicated play dates for your tasks. You allocate specific chunks of your day to focus solely on one thing, whether it's answering emails, working on a project, or even taking a breather. By knowing exactly when you'll tackle each task, you can dive in with laser focus, knowing that everything has its time and place. Single-tasking is its trusty sidekick. Instead of flipping between tasks like a restless channel surfer, stick with one until it's done. This laser focus means less switching costs, which is just a fancy way of saying you don't waste time getting back into the groove. It's like maintaining a steady rhythm rather than a chaotic drum solo.

Regular breaks are the unsung heroes of productivity. Ever tried to sprint a marathon? Yeah, neither have I, (I watch my wife doing that instead :)) and there's a reason for that. It's exhausting! Your brain works the same way. After intense periods of focus, it needs a breather to recharge. Taking regular breaks is like hitting the pause button, letting your mind wander and refresh before diving back into the fray. A five-minute walk, a quick stretch, or even a moment of meditation can do wonders for your mental energy. These breaks aren't just downtime; they're vital pit stops that keep you running smoothly, preventing burnout and boosting creativity.

To help keep your productivity zen-like, there are tools and apps designed to support mindful work. Digital calendars are your new best friends, helping you schedule those all-important breaks and block out time for focused work. Apps like Focus@Will provide background music scientifically designed to reduce distractions and enhance concentration. They're like having a personal DJ who knows just what tune will get you into the zone. Using these tools is like having a productivity coach whispering in your ear, reminding you to stay on track and take those much-needed breaks.

Lastly, seek balance in how you approach your work. Prioritize tasks not just by what's urgent but by what's truly important. It's like deciding whether to tackle the laundry or the leaky roof first—one can wait, the other might lead to a soggy mess. Allow for flexibility in task management. Life happens, and sometimes your best-laid plans will need a little wiggle room. Being adaptable ensures that you stay productive without stressing over things beyond your control. It's about finding a rhythm that works for you, allowing you to be productive without feeling overwhelmed.

Setting Boundaries: Protecting Your Mental Health

Ever felt like you're a sponge, soaking up everyone else's problems until you're ready to burst? That's where boundaries step in, acting like a protective shield for your mental health. They're crucial for keeping burnout and stress at bay. Think of them as the invisible fence that keeps the chaos from trampling your mental garden. Without boundaries, you're liable to become overwhelmed and stretched thin as you try to meet everyone's demands. Too often, we end up sacrificing our mental well-being on the altar of people-pleasing, but setting boundaries is about reclaiming your peace and ensuring you have the bandwidth to care for yourself.

Healthy boundaries also play a vital role in maintaining relationships. You know that friend who always borrows your stuff and never returns it? Boundaries help you gently say, "Hey, can we talk about my missing blender?" They guide interactions, ensuring mutual respect and understanding. When you've clearly defined what's okay and what's not, it's easier to nurture relationships that are fulfilling rather than draining. Boundaries aren't about putting up walls—they're about setting up guardrails that keep interactions respectful and mutually beneficial.

So, how do you go about setting these boundaries effectively? Start by identifying your personal limits and needs, just like a gardener deciding which plants to keep and which weeds to pull out. Reflect on what makes you uncomfortable, stressed, or resentful. These feelings are often red flags, signalling areas where boundaries might be lacking. Once you've identified these areas, communicate your boundaries assertively and respectfully. It's not about being confrontational; it's about being clear. Use "I" statements to express how certain actions affect you, like, "I need some quiet time after work to recharge, so I'll be turning my phone off for an hour."

Now, setting boundaries is one thing, but maintaining them? That's where the real challenge lies. Guilt can sneak in, whispering sweet nothings about how you're being selfish or unreasonable. It's important to remember that taking care of yourself isn't selfish; it's necessary. Dealing with pushback from others can also test your resolve. People might not like the change, especially if they're used to having unfiltered access to your time and energy. However, reinforcing your boundaries consistently is key. It's like training a puppy—patience and consistency are your best friends. Stick to your boundaries, even when it's uncomfortable, and over time, others will adjust.

Real-life scenarios can illustrate the power of effective boundaries. Take the workplace, for example. You're drowning in tasks, and your boss asks you to take on another project. It's tempting to say yes to appear accommodating, but you decide to protect your mental health instead. You say, "I'd love to help, but I'm at capacity right now. Can we discuss redistributing some of my current tasks?" Or consider social commitments. You're invited to yet another weekend event, but you're craving some alone time. You politely decline, explaining that you need some downtime to recharge. These examples show that boundaries can be set without burning bridges.

Boundaries, when set and maintained, can transform your mental landscape. They give you the freedom to focus on what truly matters, ensuring your mental well-being remains intact amidst the demands of daily life.

Managing Relationships: Navigating Social Stressors

Ah, relationships—the double-edged sword of life. On one hand, they can be the source of immense joy, while on the other, they can stir up stress like nothing else. Social stressors often come from conflicts in personal or work relationships. Picture a tense meeting at work where everyone's on edge, or a misunderstanding with a friend that spirals out of control. These conflicts are common culprits, turning peaceful interactions into battlegrounds. Then there's the pressure to meet social expectations, which can feel like wearing a suit two sizes too small. Whether it's attending every social gathering or maintaining a picture-perfect life on social media, the weight of these expectations can be crushing.

Navigating these social stressors requires some finesse. Start with active listening and empathetic communication. It's about truly hearing the other person, not just waiting for your turn to speak. When someone talks, focus on their words, their tone, and what they're not saying. It's like tuning into a radio station where the music is more important than the static. Empathy comes into play when you try to understand their perspective, even if you don't agree. Maybe your colleague snapped at you because they're overwhelmed, or your friend cancelled plans because they're going through a rough patch. By putting yourself in their shoes, you create space for understanding and resolution.

Conflict resolution skills are your toolkit for defusing tense situations. Imagine a heated conversation as a tangled ball of yarn. Your job is to gently tease out each thread until it's manageable. Start by acknowledging the issue and expressing your feelings without blame. Use "I" statements to own your emotions, like, "I felt hurt when plans changed last minute." Then, work collaboratively to find a solution that respects both parties' needs. It's like building a bridge rather than a barrier, ensuring everyone feels heard and valued.

Social support is the secret sauce that helps manage stress. Build a network of trusted confidants—people who have your back, no matter what. They're the ones you can call in the middle of the night when you need to vent or celebrate. A strong support system acts like a safety net, catching you when social stressors threaten to knock you down. Sometimes, leaning on mental health professionals is also crucial. Therapists and counsellors provide an objective perspective, offering strategies to navigate complex relationships and emotional challenges.

Maintaining healthy relationships requires consistent effort and mutual understanding. Regular check-ins with loved ones keep the lines of communication open. It's like regularly tuning your car to keep it running smoothly. Ask how they're doing, share your thoughts, and discuss any niggling issues before they snowball. Setting mutual expectations and agreements is like drawing a map for your relationships, ensuring everyone knows where they stand. Maybe that means agreeing to unplug during dinner or setting aside time for a weekly catch-up. These practices create a foundation of trust and respect, nurturing connections that withstand the test of time.

Navigating social stressors is an ongoing dance, requiring patience, empathy, and a willingness to adapt. While conflicts and pressures will always exist, how you handle them can make all the difference. By honing your communication skills, seeking support, and maintaining healthy practices, you can turn potential stressors into opportunities for growth and connection. Relationships, after all, are the heartbeats that add rhythm to our lives, and managing them well leads to a symphony of harmony and understanding.

Self-Compassion: The Antidote to Guilt and Self-Doubt

Ever caught yourself being your own worst critic, replaying every little mistake like a broken record? Welcome to the club. But let's talk about self-compassion, the secret sauce for turning that harsh inner critic into a gentle coach. Self-compassion is all about treating yourself with the same kindness and understanding you'd offer a close friend. Imagine your best friend coming to you, feeling down after a bad day. You wouldn't point out all their flaws or remind them of their failures. Instead, you'd offer a listening ear, some comforting words, and maybe even a cheeky joke to lighten the mood. That's self-compassion in a nutshell. It's about being your own ally, not your own enemy.

Now, it's important to distinguish self-compassion from self-indulgence. Self-compassion doesn't mean letting yourself off the hook for everything or ignoring responsibilities. It's not about eating cake for breakfast every day or avoiding difficult conversations. Instead, it's about recognising that everyone makes mistakes and that imperfection is part of being human. It's understanding that while you might have fallen short today, it doesn't define your worth. Self-compassion is the gentle reminder that you're doing your best and that it's okay to stumble now and then. It's the antidote to self-doubt and guilt, those pesky emotions that love to rear their heads when you least expect them.

So, how does self-compassion work its magic on these negative emotions? For starters, it helps reduce feelings of guilt and inadequacy. When you're kind to yourself, you're less likely to dwell on past mistakes or beat yourself up over things beyond your control. Instead, you become more resilient, bouncing back from setbacks with renewed strength. Self-compassion enhances emotional resilience, fortifying you against the storms of life. It's like a warm blanket on a cold day, offering comfort and strength when you need it most. With self-compassion, you can face challenges head-on, knowing that you have the inner resources to cope.

Practising self-compassion doesn't require a complete lifestyle overhaul. Start small with self-compassionate journaling exercises. Write down your thoughts and feelings, but instead of criticising yourself, approach them with curiosity and kindness. Ask yourself what you'd say to a friend in your situation, and write that down. Let your journal be a safe space where you can explore your emotions without judgment. Another technique is mindful self-talk. Notice when you're being hard on yourself, and consciously change the narrative. Replace

"I'm such a failure" with "I'm learning, and that's okay." It might feel awkward at first, but over time, these small shifts in language can make a big difference in how you perceive yourself.

Integrating self-compassion into daily life is about setting realistic expectations. No one's perfect, and expecting yourself to be flawless is a recipe for disappointment. Instead, celebrate personal achievements and progress, no matter how small. Did you finally tackle that dreaded task at work? Treat yourself to a small reward. Managed to squeeze in a workout despite a hectic schedule? Give yourself a mental high-five. These moments of acknowledgement reinforce positive behaviour and remind you that you're moving forward, even if it's one tiny step at a time. It's about recognising that progress is progress, and every step counts.

Self-compassion is a journey of self-discovery, an ongoing practice that requires patience and persistence. But the rewards are well worth the effort. With self-compassion, you cultivate a sense of inner peace and resilience, empowering yourself to face life's challenges with grace and strength. It's about being kind to yourself, not just when you succeed but especially when you stumble. So, next time you find yourself spiralling into self-doubt, pause, take a deep breath, and remember to treat yourself with the kindness and understanding you truly deserve.

Creating a Supportive Environment: Building Your Tribe

Imagine life as a long-distance marathon. You're pacing yourself, managing the hills and valleys, but it's the people cheering from the sidelines who make the difference. Having a supportive environment is like having your personal fan club, encouraging you to keep going when you'd rather just collapse on the couch. This environment isn't just a nice-to-have; it's crucial for mental health. It offers encouragement and motivation when your internal pep talks fall flat. It's where you find shared experiences and resources, like a treasure trove of wisdom and support that you didn't even know you needed. Whether it's advice on navigating tough times or just a friendly ear to listen, a supportive community wraps you in a warm embrace of understanding.

Building this network might seem daunting, especially if you're used to flying solo. But here's a little secret: you're not alone in feeling alone. Many people are seeking connection, just like you. Start by joining interest-based groups or clubs. Whether it's a book club, a sports team, or a knitting circle, these gatherings are fertile ground for friendships to bloom. It's where like-minded individuals gather, sharing not just hobbies but camaraderie. Reaching out to these groups is like planting seeds in a garden—you might not see results overnight, but with a little nurturing, you'll soon be surrounded by a lush network of support.

The role of the community in mental health is profound. It offers a sense of belonging and connection, a reminder that you're part of something bigger than yourself. Engaging with a community gives you the chance to both give and receive support. It's a two-way street where collaboration and mutual aid thrive. You help others, and in turn, you find help when you need it. It's like a safety net woven from the threads of shared experiences and understanding. This connection reduces feelings of isolation, replacing them with a sense of purpose and belonging. When you engage with your community, you tap into a wellspring of strength and resilience that's far greater than the sum of its parts.

Being part of a community isn't just about showing up; it's about active participation. Attend community events or meetings where you can connect with others face-to-face and build relationships beyond the digital realm. Volunteering for community projects or initiatives is another powerful way to engage. It's a chance to give back while also expanding your network. These activities not only strengthen your ties but also enrich your life with new perspectives and experiences. They're like adding vibrant threads to the tapestry of your life, each one contributing to the rich, diverse pattern of your story.

Building a supportive environment is about creating a tribe that stands by you through thick and thin. It's not just about having people around; it's about forging connections that uplift and inspire you. These relationships are the roots that anchor you, providing stability and nourishment as you navigate life's challenges. They remind you that, no matter how tough things get, you're never truly alone. By actively engaging with your community, you cultivate a support system that nurtures your mental health and enriches your life. It's this sense of belonging and connection that fortifies you, empowering you to face whatever comes your way with courage and confidence.

EIGHT

Sustaining Long-Term Mental Health

I magine you're trying to grow a lush garden. You plant the seeds, water them once, and then sit back, expecting a garden of Eden to sprout overnight. But you know what happens? The weeds take over, and the plants barely survive, let alone thrive. That's the thing about quick fixes—they're like expecting a seed to become a full-grown tree with just one splash of water. When it comes to mental health, quick fixes might give you a brief sense of relief, a bit like that instant high from a sugar rush, but the crash isn't far behind. They're Band-Aids, not cures. They provide temporary comfort, but they don't address the root of the issue. You might find your-self reaching for the same superficial solutions repeatedly, which can lead to dependency. Who wants to be stuck in that loop when there's a better, more sustainable way?

Now, let's talk about the long game. It's the slow, steady watering and nurturing of those seeds. Mental health improvement is a marathon, not a sprint. Embracing incremental progress is key. Picture this: every small step you take, every little change you make, is like adding another brick to your mental health fortress. Over time, these bricks accumulate to form a strong foundation. Setting long-term goals can keep you on track. Think of them as the North Star guiding you through the fog. It's not about making huge leaps; it's about those consistent, tiny steps forward. Like learning to play an instrument, it's not about mastering a symphony overnight but practising a few notes every day until you can play a full piece.

Commitment and patience are your best buddies on this journey. Mental health doesn't transform overnight, and that's okay. Progress takes time, just like it takes time to bake a cake. Rushing it only leads to a gooey mess, and nobody wants that. Building resilience through consistent effort is what will see you through the tough spots. It's like training for a marathon. Some days, you'll feel like you're running through a fog, while other days, you'll feel like you're flying. The key is to keep putting one foot in front of the other, trusting that each step is making you stronger.

Real-life stories can be incredibly inspiring in this context. Take Sarah, for instance. She faced severe anxiety for years, relying on short-term fixes like excessive caffeine for energy and avoidance tactics to cope. But things changed when she decided to focus on long-term strategies. She started with small, manageable goals, like attending a weekly yoga class and practising mindfulness for five minutes a day. Over months, these tiny changes built up, and she noticed a profound shift. Sarah's story is a testament to the power of gradual transformation. Or consider James, who struggled with depression. Instead of looking for quick solutions, he dedicated himself to therapy and regular exercise. It took time, but with commitment, James found himself in a much healthier place emotionally and mentally.

Interactive Element: Reflection on Personal Progress

Take a moment to reflect on your own mental health journey. What small, consistent steps have you taken that have positively impacted your well-being over time? Write down your thoughts and consider how these steps have contributed to your overall mental health.

These stories aren't just anecdotes; they're roadmaps. They show that with patience and perseverance, you can achieve long-term mental health success. It's about focusing on the long haul, committing to the process, and being kind to yourself along the way. Your mental health garden may take time to flourish, but when it does, it's a beautiful sight to behold.

Building Lasting Habits: Strategies for Consistency

Picture this: you're trying to build a new habit, like flossing every night or going for a morning jog. You start strong, but then life happens—a late night at work, an unexpected visit from a friend—and before you know it, you're back to your old ways. Don't worry, you're not alone. The struggle to maintain habits is as common as finding a sock monster in your laundry. The secret lies in understanding the habit loop, a concept that breaks down habits into three parts: cue, routine, and reward. The cue is what triggers the habit, like seeing your running shoes by the door. The routine is the action itself, like going for that jog. And the reward is the satisfaction or benefit you get, like feeling more energetic throughout the day. Knowing this loop can help you design habits that stick because once a routine is established, your brain requires less effort to keep it going. Repetition is key here—when you do something repeatedly, it becomes automatic, like driving a car without thinking about every little action.

Now, let's talk about strategies to make those habits stick like glue. Ever heard of habit stacking? It's like piggybacking a new habit onto an existing one. Say you already have a morning coffee ritual. You could stack a quick meditation session right after your first sip. The existing habit acts as a cue for the new one, making it easier to remember. Reminders and prompts can also work wonders. Set alarms on your phone or leave sticky notes in strategic places. They're gentle nudges that keep you on track, like a friendly tap on the shoulder reminding you to call your mum. Consistency is the magic ingredient in habit formation. It's not about being perfect but about showing up, even if it's imperfect.

But let's be real: life throws curveballs. Setbacks and slip-ups happen. They're like surprise potholes on your road to success. The key is not to let them derail your entire journey. Instead of throwing in the towel after a missed day, acknowledge the slip and get back on track. Adapting habits to life changes is crucial. Maybe your routine needs tweaking because of a new job or a change in family dynamics. Flexibility is your ally here. Reevaluate and adjust your habits to fit your current lifestyle rather than forcing yourself into an outdated mould.

Regular reflection on your habits is like checking the map while you're driving. It helps you see if you're still headed in the right direction or if a detour is needed. Track your progress, whether it's through a journal, an app, or even a simple chart on the fridge. Not only does this show how far you've come, but it also highlights areas for improvement. And don't forget to celebrate your consistency and persistence. Every small victory is worth acknowledging, like hitting a milestone in a video game. It reinforces the behaviour and keeps you motivated.

Interactive Element: Habit Reflection Exercise

Take some time to reflect on a habit you're working to build. What's the cue that nudges you to start? Consider the routine you follow and the reward you receive afterwards. It can be really beneficial to find ways to make the routine feel more enjoyable or to enhance the reward so it feels more fulfilling. Take a moment to jot down your thoughts, and think about any small changes you might want to implement. Remember, the journey of creating new habits can be quite an uplifting experience, so be gentle and compassionate with yourself as you navigate this process!

Building lasting habits is about creating a life that aligns with your goals and values. It's about crafting routines that support your mental health and well-being, rather than working against them. With a little patience, a dash of creativity, and a lot of consistency, you can turn those fledgling habits into a foundation for a healthier, more balanced life.

The Role of Neuroplasticity: Rewiring Your Brain for Better Health

Imagine your brain is a bustling city, teeming with highways of thoughts and backstreets of memories. Neuroplasticity is the city's ability to rebuild, adapt, and reorganize itself in response to its experiences. It's like the brain's version of a personal trainer, constantly reshaping itself based on what it encounters. This adaptability is crucial for learning and behaviour change. If you've ever picked up a new skill or broken an old habit, you've witnessed neuroplasticity in action. It's the brain's way of saying, "Hey, I can change!" This process allows us to form new connections and pathways, making it possible to adapt to new situations or recover from setbacks.

When it comes to mental health, neuroplasticity is a game-changer. It offers a glimmer of hope that no matter how entrenched certain thought patterns might seem, they can be altered. This adaptability can help reduce symptoms of anxiety and depression by encouraging the brain to form new, healthier paths. Imagine your mind as a garden overgrown with weeds of negativity. Neuroplasticity acts as the gardener, helping to clear out those weeds and plant seeds of positivity and resilience. Developing new thought patterns through neuroplasticity means you're not stuck in a mental rut; you're capable of change and growth.

One effective way to enhance neuroplasticity is through mindfulness meditation. This isn't just about sitting cross-legged on a cushion and chanting "om." It's about training your brain to focus, breathe, and be present. Mindfulness meditation can help rewire the brain by strengthening connections in areas associated with attention and emotional regulation. It's like hitting the reset button on your mental circuitry, allowing you to approach life with a clearer, calmer mindset. Cognitive-behavioural exercises are another tool in your neuroplasticity toolkit. They challenge you to identify and change negative thought patterns, rewiring your brain to think more positively. It's like upgrading your brain's operating system, helping it run more smoothly and efficiently.

Let's take a look at some real-life success stories. Meet Emily, who struggled with persistent anxiety. Through mindfulness meditation and cognitive exercises, she noticed significant improvements in her mental health. Emily described it as if her brain was a tangled ball of yarn that slowly began to unravel and straighten out. She found herself more focused, less reactive, and better able to handle stress. Her experience is just one of many examples of how neuroplasticity can lead to cognitive transformation. Research studies back this up, showing that regular meditation can increase grey matter in the brain areas responsible for memory, learning, and emotional regulation. These findings offer a powerful reminder of the brain's incredible capacity for change.

Neuroplasticity is more than just a scientific concept; it's a beacon of hope for those seeking to improve their mental health. It's a testament to the brain's resilience and adaptability, proving that change is possible at any age. Whether you're looking to break free from anxiety, lift the fog of depression, or simply enhance your mental agility, neuroplasticity provides the framework for a healthier, more balanced mind.

Gratitude and Positivity: Shifting Focus for Greater Happiness

Gratitude. It's like the unsung hero in the mental health playbook, quietly working backstage to keep everything running smoothly. When you focus on gratitude, you start seeing life through a different lens. It's not about ignoring the tough stuff but rather shifting your gaze to the good bits, like finding a hidden gem in the midst of chaos. Gratitude helps reroute your thoughts from dwelling on the negatives to appreciating the positives. It acts like a mental compass, steering you toward a more optimistic outlook. Imagine waking up each day and choosing to notice what's going right. That shift can be nothing short of transformative. It's like opening the curtains to let the sunlight pour in, instantly brightening the room.

So, how do you practice gratitude? Start with a gratitude journal. Each day, jot down three things you're thankful for. It doesn't need to be something grand; even small joys count. Maybe it's the smell of fresh coffee or a text from an old friend. This simple exercise rewires your brain to notice and appreciate the positives in your life. Another practice is sharing gratitude with others through letters. Write a note to someone who's made a difference in your life. You don't even have to send it—just the act of writing can boost your mood and strengthen your emotional connections. It's a bit like sending a mental thank you card, which lifts both your spirits and theirs.

Now, let's talk about positive thinking. It's not about wearing rose-coloured glasses and ignoring reality. It's about reframing challenges as opportunities to learn and grow. Life throws curveballs, sure, but a positive mindset helps you catch them with grace. Positive affirmations can be powerful tools here. Start your day by affirming your strengths and abilities. It might feel a bit awkward at first, like talking to yourself in the mirror, but over time, it can shift your self-perception. Imagine starting each day with a pep talk that fuels your confidence and sets a positive tone.

The long-term benefits of gratitude and positivity are profound. They act like mental armour, bolstering your resilience to stress. When you cultivate gratitude, it's like building a reservoir of positivity that you can draw from during tough times. Relationships also flourish under the influence of gratitude. Seeing the good in others fosters deeper connections and empathy, transforming the way you interact. It's like adding a splash of colour to your relationships, making them more vibrant and fulfilling. Overall, gratitude and positivity weave a safety net of emotional well-being, allowing you to navigate life with a sense of grace and strength.

Reflection Exercise: Daily Gratitude Journal

Take a few minutes each evening to reflect on your day. Write down or say out loud three things you're grateful for, no matter how small. Notice how this practice shifts your focus and enhances your well-being over time.

Embracing Life's Journey: Finding Joy in the Everyday

Imagine finding little pockets of joy sprinkled throughout your day, like discovering extra fries at the bottom of the bag. Joy isn't some elusive unicorn that only shows up on special occasions. It's a vital part of our emotional toolkit, a secret ingredient that keeps our mental health soup from becoming bland. When joy is present, it acts as a buoy, lifting us up and making us more resilient to life's downturns. It's like wearing emotional armour, deflecting stress and negativity. Joy's impact isn't just a fleeting mood booster; it's a cornerstone of emotional resilience. It strengthens our overall well-being, making the challenges we face seem a bit more manageable and a lot less daunting.

One way to cultivate this joy is through mindfulness, which sounds fancy but is really about paying attention. Not the kind of attention you give in a boring meeting, but the kind you give to your favourite song. Engaging fully in daily activities, whether it's savouring your morning coffee or listening to a friend, anchors you in the present. This presence turns ordinary moments into extraordinary ones, like finding hidden treasures in everyday life. Nature can also be a great teacher of mindfulness. Take a walk and observe the world around you, from the rustling leaves to the chirping birds. It's like watching a live documentary, reminding you of the beauty that's often overlooked in the rush of daily life.

Incorporating more joy into your life can start with identifying small pleasures and enjoying them like a fine wine. It could be the first sip of coffee in the morning or the sound of rain tapping on the window. Create rituals that bring joy and meaning, like a weekly movie night or a morning dance party in your kitchen. These rituals become anchors in your day, giving you something to look forward to, a moment to relish. It's about weaving joy into the fabric of your daily routine, not just reserving it for special occasions. It's like having a secret stash of happiness that you can dip into whenever you need a boost.

Embracing joy can transform your entire mental health experience. It leads to greater satisfaction and contentment, providing a sense of fulfilment that transcends temporary happiness. Joy also enhances creativity and problem-solving. When you're in a joyful state, your mind opens up, seeing possibilities and solutions that were once hidden. It's like turning on a light in a dark room, revealing paths you hadn't noticed before. This creative spark can lead to better decision-making and a more vibrant life. Joy is not just an emotion; it's a way of being in the world, a choice to find beauty and meaning in the mundane.

Reflection Exercise: Finding Joy in the Everyday

Take a moment each evening to reflect on the joyful moments you experienced during the day. Write them down in a journal, no matter how small or simple they may seem. Notice how this practice shifts your focus and enhances your overall sense of well-being.

When you make the conscious choice to embrace joy, you create a ripple effect in your life. It colours your interactions with others, making relationships richer and more fulfilling. It infuses your day with moments of lightness and laughter, breaking up the monotony and stress that can sometimes weigh us down. Emphasising joy doesn't mean ignoring the tough stuff; it means acknowledging it while also celebrating the good. It's about finding balance, like a tightrope walker who finds steadiness amidst the sway. Joy is always there, waiting to be discovered in the little things.

Your Mental Health Legacy: Inspiring Others with Your Story

Sharing your mental health story is a bit like showing up to a costume party dressed as yourself. It's raw, it's real, and it might be scary, but it's also incredibly liberating. When you open up about your experiences, you're not just talking about yourself; you're lighting a path for others who might be wandering in the dark. Imagine someone out there, feeling alone with their struggles, stumbling upon your story. Suddenly, they're not alone anymore. Your vulnerability becomes a beacon of hope, a reminder that healing is possible. By sharing your journey, you dismantle the stigma surrounding mental health brick by brick, fostering a world where understanding flourishes.

But sharing your story does more than inspire others; it creates a ripple effect, building a community of support and empathy. Storytelling is a powerful tool for connection. It's like a bridge, linking you to others who have faced similar challenges. When you share, you invite others to do the same.

It's a way of saying, "I see you, and I understand." This openness encourages vulnerability, creating a safe space where people can express their feelings without fear of judgment. In a world that often feels disconnected, these stories weave a tapestry of shared experiences, binding us together with threads of empathy.

If you're wondering how to start, don't worry—I've got your back. Effective storytelling is more than just recounting events; it's about sharing the lessons you've learned and the growth you've experienced. Focus on the transformation, the moments that shaped you, and the insights that emerged from your struggles. These are the stories that resonate, offering guidance and inspiration. Platforms like blogs or social media can be great places to share your journey. They allow you to reach a wider audience, spreading your message to those who most need it. Whether you write a heartfelt post on Facebook or start a blog, the key is authenticity. Speak from the heart, and let your voice be heard.

Becoming a mental health advocate is like planting seeds of change in the world. As you share your story, you empower others to seek help to support. Your voice becomes part of a broader movement for mental health awareness, contributing to a cultural shift that values understanding and compassion. Advocacy isn't just about raising awareness; it's about making an impact. It's about creating a world where mental health is prioritised and where stigma has no place. By sharing your experiences, you become a catalyst for change, inspiring others to take steps toward their own healing and growth.

This chapter explored how sharing your mental health story can inspire others and create a supportive community. Your story is more than just words; it's a legacy that leaves a lasting impact, empowering others and contributing to a movement for mental health awareness. As we move forward, let's continue to embrace vulnerability and foster understanding, creating a world where mental health is celebrated, and stigma is a thing of the past. #itsokaynottobeokay

I came to write this book with no real understanding of how profound it would be in <u>my</u> life. I had come to a point where I was losing my job and had no income and direction, but I still had a mortgage and bills to pay. WTF, no one said it would be this hard; is about me noticing that no one told me how life could be so unforgiving and, worse, how mean I was to my own mental health. If you wouldn't say these things to anyone suffering how I was feeling, why do we say them in our head to ourselves? Over time a long time, I have tried counselling of many flavours and varieties and hypnosis and workshops and many journals that I never kept up with, and what I've discovered is that we need a bit of everything, really. But this is your adventure. Make it a good one, fill your bag with tools you can use, and discard the ones you don't. No one can say it's wrong; it's personal, and I hope I am with you every step of the way. I may not know or recognise your story, but I sure as hell recognise the feelings that go with it. #itsokaynottobeokay

Thank you for reading my book.

References

The Importance of Mental Health Awareness | Wake Forest ... https://counseling.online.wfu.edu/blog/how-mental-health-stigmas-are-changing/

Busted: 7 myths about mental health https://www.unicef.org/parenting/health/busted-7-myths-about-mental-health

How to Build a Support System For Your Mental Health https://mywellbeing.com/therapy-101/how-to-build-a-support-system

The Best Mental Health Apps, Tried and Tested https://www.verywellmind.com/best-mental-health-apps-4692902

The Connection Between Self-Care and Mental Health https://www.psychologytoday.com/us/blog/a-deeper-wellness/202302/understanding-the-mental-health-and-self-care-connection

18 Self-Care Tips for Busy People – Georgia HOPE https://gahope.org/18-self-care-tips-for-busy-people/

Mindfulness exercises https://www.mayoclinic.org/healthy-lifestyle/consumer-health/in-depth/mindfulness-exercises/art-20046356

Impacts of digital social media detox for mental health - PubMed https://pubmed.ncbi.nlm.nih.gov/39280291/#:

Review of Grit and Resilience Literature within Health ... https://pmc.ncbi.nlm.nih.gov/articles/PMC5869747/#:

10 Inspiring Stories of People Who Overcame Adversity https://listverse.com/2023/05/14/10-inspiring-stories-of-people-who-overcame-adversity/

Nurturing Growth Mindsets: Six Tips From Carol Dweck https://www.edweek.org/leadership/nurturing-growth-mindsets-six-tips-from-carol-dweck/2016/03

Neuroscientist: Do these 6 exercises every day to build ... https://www.cnbc.com/2021/08/31/do-these-exercises-every-day-to-build-resilience-and-mental-strength-says-neuroscientist.html

Psychotherapies - National Institute of Mental Health (NIMH) https://www.nimh.nih.gov/health/topics/psychotherapies

A step-by-step guide to finding a therapist https://www.npr.org/sections/health-shots/2023/07/02/1185661348/start-therapy-find-therapist-how-to

9 Ways to Fight Mental Health Stigma | NAMI https://www.

nami.org/Blogs/NAMI-Blog/October-2017/9-Ways-to-Fight-Mental-Health-Stigma

Integrating self-help and psychotherapy. - APA PsycNet https://psycnet.apa.org/record/2019-28355-017

Primary and Secondary Emotions: What's The Difference? https://www.simplypsychology.org/primary-and-secondary-emotions.html

What's the difference between stress and anxiety? https://www.apa.org/topics/stress/anxiety-difference

10 Ways to Boost Your Emotional Resilience, Backed by ... https://time.com/4306492/boost-emotional-resilience/

The Power of Emotional Intelligence in Relationships https://care-clinics.com/the-power-of-emotional-intelligence-in-relationships/

How To Develop A Personal Growth Mindset That Fuels ... https://www.forbes.com/councils/forbesbusinessdevelopmentcouncil/2020/12/21/how-to-develop-a-personal-growth-mindset-that-fuels-business-success/

How to Set and Use SMART Goals https://www.verywellmind.com/smart-goals-for-lifestyle-change-2224097

8 Ways to Practice Self-Reflection: A Path to Personal Growth https://www.talktoangel.com/blog/8-ways-to-practice-self-reflection-a-path-to-personal-growth

How to Cope With the Fear of Change https://www.verywellmind.com/i-fear-change-how-to-cope-with-the-unknown-5189851

Why is Work-Life Balance Important for Mental Health? https://vervebh.com/why-is-work-life-balance-important-for-mental-health/

5 Ways Mindfulness Can Increase Your Productivity https://www.forbes.com/sites/tracybrower/2024/10/28/how-5-mindfulness-techniques-can-help-your-workplace-productivity/

Setting Healthy Boundaries: A Key to Improving Mental ... https://www.recoveryways.com/rehab-blog/setting-healthy-boundaries-a-key-to-improving-mental-health/

The Role of Community in Our Mental Health | Samaritans https://samaritanshope.org/community-education-outreach/the-role-of-community-in-our-mental-health/

Long-Term Strategies for Sustaining Mental Health https://southcoastcounselorsandphysicians.com/long-term-strategies-for-sustaining-mental-health/

Habits: How They Form And How To Break Them https://www.npr.org/2012/03/05/147192599/habits-how-they-form-and-how-to-break-them

Applying the Principles of Neuroplasticity to Improve ... https://www.axismh.

com/post/applying-the-principles-of-neuroplasticity-to-improve-mental-health

Rance, L. (2018). Achieve New Year's resolution with good food. Winnipeg Free Press, (), C7.

How Gratitude Changes You and Your Brain https://greatergood.berkeley.edu/article/item/how_gratitude_changes_you_and_your_brain

https://www.calm.com

https://headspace.com

https://mindvalley.com

Printed in Great Britain
by Amazon